Mometrix
TEST PREPARATION

New York
State Tests
Grade 4
Science
Success Strategies

DEAR FUTURE EXAM SUCCESS STORY

First of all, **THANK YOU** for purchasing Mometrix study materials!

Second, congratulations! You are one of the few determined test-takers who are committed to doing whatever it takes to excel on your exam. **You have come to the right place.** We developed these study materials with one goal in mind: to deliver you the information you need in a format that's concise and easy to use.

In addition to optimizing your guide for the content of the test, we've outlined our recommended steps for breaking down the preparation process into small, attainable goals so you can make sure you stay on track.

We've also analyzed the entire test-taking process, identifying the most common pitfalls and showing how you can overcome them and be ready for any curveball the test throws you.

Standardized testing is one of the biggest obstacles on your road to success, which only increases the importance of doing well in the high-pressure, high-stakes environment of test day. Your results on this test could have a significant impact on your future, and this guide provides the information and practical advice to help you achieve your full potential on test day.

Your success is our success

We would love to hear from you! If you would like to share the story of your exam success or if you have any questions or comments in regard to our products, please contact us at **800-673-8175** or **support@mometrix.com**.

Thanks again for your business and we wish you continued success!

Sincerely,
The Mometrix Test Preparation Team

Need more help? Check out our flashcards at: http://MometrixFlashcards.com/STAAR

TABLE OF CONTENTS

Introduction

Thank you for purchasing this resource! You have made the choice to prepare yourself for a test that could have a huge impact on your future, and this guide is designed to help you be fully ready for test day. Obviously, it's important to have a solid understanding of the test material, but you also need to be prepared for the unique environment and stressors of the test, so that you can perform to the best of your abilities.

For this purpose, the first section that appears in this guide is the **Success Strategies**. We've devoted countless hours to meticulously researching what works and what doesn't, and we've boiled down our findings to the five most impactful steps you can take to improve your performance on the test. We start at the beginning with study planning and move through the preparation process, all the way to the testing strategies that will help you get the most out of what you know when you're finally sitting in front of the test.

We recommend that you start preparing for your test as far in advance as possible. However, if you've bought this guide as a last-minute study resource and only have a few days before your test, we recommend that you skip over the first two Success Strategies since they address a long-term study plan.

If you struggle with **test anxiety**, we strongly encourage you to check out our recommendations for how you can overcome it. Test anxiety is a formidable foe, but it can be beaten, and we want to make sure you have the tools you need to defeat it.

Strategy #1 – Plan Big, Study Small

There's a lot riding on your performance. If you want to ace this test, you're going to need to keep your skills sharp and the material fresh in your mind. You need a plan that lets you review everything you need to know while still fitting in your schedule. We'll break this strategy down into three categories.

Information Organization

Start with the information you already have: the official test outline. From this, you can make a complete list of all the concepts you need to cover before the test. Organize these concepts into groups that can be studied together, and create a list of any related vocabulary you need to learn so you can brush up on any difficult terms. You'll want to keep this vocabulary list handy once you actually start studying since you may need to add to it along the way.

Time Management

Once you have your set of study concepts, decide how to spread them out over the time you have left before the test. Break your study plan into small, clear goals so you have a manageable task for each day and know exactly what you're doing. Then just focus on one small step at a time. When you manage your time this way, you don't need to spend hours at a time studying. Studying a small block of content for a short period each day helps you retain information better and avoid stressing over how much you have left to do. You can relax knowing that you have a plan to cover everything in time. In order for this strategy to be effective though, you have to start studying early and stick to your schedule. Avoid the exhaustion and futility that comes from last-minute cramming!

Study Environment

The environment you study in has a big impact on your learning. Studying in a coffee shop, while probably more enjoyable, is not likely to be as fruitful as studying in a quiet room. It's important to keep distractions to a minimum. You're only planning to study for a short block of time, so make the most of it. Don't pause to check your phone or get up to find a snack. It's also important to **avoid multitasking**. Research has consistently shown that multitasking will make your studying dramatically less effective. Your study area should also be comfortable and well-lit so you don't have the distraction of straining your eyes or sitting on an uncomfortable chair.

 The time of day you study is also important. You want to be rested and alert. Don't wait until just before bedtime. Study when you'll be most likely to comprehend and remember. Even better, if you know what time of day your test will be, set that time aside for study. That way your brain will be used to working on that subject at that specific time and you'll have a better chance of recalling information.

Finally, it can be helpful to team up with others who are studying for the same test. Your actual studying should be done in as isolated an environment as possible, but the work of organizing the information and setting up the study plan can be divided up. In between study sessions, you can discuss with your teammates the concepts that you're all studying and quiz each other on the details. Just be sure that your teammates are as serious about the test as you are. If you find that your study time is being replaced with social time, you might need to find a new team.

Strategy #2 – Make Your Studying Count

You're devoting a lot of time and effort to preparing for this test, so you want to be absolutely certain it will pay off. This means doing more than just reading the content and hoping you can remember it on test day. It's important to make every minute of study count. There are two main areas you can focus on to make your studying count.

Retention

It doesn't matter how much time you study if you can't remember the material. You need to make sure you are retaining the concepts. To check your retention of the information you're learning, try recalling it at later times with minimal prompting. Try carrying around flashcards and glance at one or two from time to time or ask a friend who's also studying for the test to quiz you.

To enhance your retention, look for ways to put the information into practice so that you can apply it rather than simply recalling it. If you're using the information in practical ways, it will be much easier to remember. Similarly, it helps to solidify a concept in your mind if you're not only reading it to yourself but also explaining it to someone else. Ask a friend to let you teach them about a concept you're a little shaky on (or speak aloud to an imaginary audience if necessary). As you try to summarize, define, give examples, and answer your friend's questions, you'll understand the concepts better and they will stay with you longer. Finally, step back for a big picture view and ask yourself how each piece of information fits with the whole subject. When you link the different concepts together and see them working together as a whole, it's easier to remember the individual components.

Finally, practice showing your work on any multi-step problems, even if you're just studying. Writing out each step you take to solve a problem will help solidify the process in your mind, and you'll be more likely to remember it during the test.

Modality

Modality simply refers to the means or method by which you study. Choosing a study modality that fits your own individual learning style is crucial. No two people learn best in exactly the same way, so it's important to know your strengths and use them to your advantage.

For example, if you learn best by visualization, focus on visualizing a concept in your mind and draw an image or a diagram. Try color-coding your notes, illustrating them, or creating symbols that will trigger your mind to recall a learned concept. If you learn best by hearing or discussing information, find a study partner who learns the same way or read aloud to yourself. Think about how to put the information in your own words. Imagine that you are giving a lecture on the topic and record yourself so you can listen to it later.

For any learning style, flashcards can be helpful. Organize the information so you can take advantage of spare moments to review. Underline key words or phrases. Use different colors for different categories. Mnemonic devices (such as creating a short list in which every item starts with the same letter) can also help with retention. Find what works best for you and use it to store the information in your mind most effectively and easily.

3

Strategy #3 – Practice the Right Way

Your success on test day depends not only on how many hours you put into preparing, but also on whether you prepared the right way. It's good to check along the way to see if your studying is paying off. One of the most effective ways to do this is by taking practice tests to evaluate your progress. Practice tests are useful because they show exactly where you need to improve. Every time you take a practice test, pay special attention to these three groups of questions:

- The questions you got wrong
- The questions you had to guess on, even if you guessed right
- The questions you found difficult or slow to work through

This will show you exactly what your weak areas are, and where you need to devote more study time. Ask yourself why each of these questions gave you trouble. Was it because you didn't understand the material? Was it because you didn't remember the vocabulary? Do you need more repetitions on this type of question to build speed and confidence? Dig into those questions and figure out how you can strengthen your weak areas as you go back to review the material.

Additionally, many practice tests have a section explaining the answer choices. It can be tempting to read the explanation and think that you now have a good understanding of the concept. However, an explanation likely only covers part of the question's broader context. Even if the explanation makes perfect sense, **go back and investigate** every concept related to the question until you're positive you have a thorough understanding.

As you go along, keep in mind that the practice test is just that: practice. Memorizing these questions and answers will not be very helpful on the actual test because it is unlikely to have any of the same exact questions. If you only know the right answers to the sample questions, you won't be prepared for the real thing. **Study the concepts** until you understand them fully, and then you'll be able to answer any question that shows up on the test.

It's important to wait on the practice tests until you're ready. If you take a test on your first day of study, you may be overwhelmed by the amount of material covered and how much you need to learn. Work up to it gradually.

On test day, you'll need to be prepared for answering questions, managing your time, and using the test-taking strategies you've learned. It's a lot to balance, like a mental marathon that will have a big impact on your future. Like training for a marathon, you'll need to start slowly and work your way up. When test day arrives, you'll be ready.

Start with the strategies you've read in the first two Success Strategies—plan your course and study in the way that works best for you. If you have time, consider using multiple study resources to get different approaches to the same concepts. It can be helpful to see difficult concepts from more than one angle. Then find a good source for practice tests. Many times, the test website will suggest potential study resources or provide sample tests.

Practice Test Strategy

If you're able to find at least three practice tests, we recommend this strategy:

UNTIMED AND OPEN-BOOK PRACTICE

Take the first test with no time constraints and with your notes and study guide handy. Take your time and focus on applying the strategies you've learned.

TIMED AND OPEN-BOOK PRACTICE

Take the second practice test open-book as well, but set a timer and practice pacing yourself to finish in time.

TIMED AND CLOSED-BOOK PRACTICE

Take any other practice tests as if it were test day. Set a timer and put away your study materials. Sit at a table or desk in a quiet room, imagine yourself at the testing center, and answer questions as quickly and accurately as possible.

Keep repeating timed and closed-book tests on a regular basis until you run out of practice tests or it's time for the actual test. Your mind will be ready for the schedule and stress of test day, and you'll be able to focus on recalling the material you've learned.

Strategy #4 – Pace Yourself

Once you're fully prepared for the material on the test, your biggest challenge on test day will be managing your time. Just knowing that the clock is ticking can make you panic even if you have plenty of time left. Work on pacing yourself so you can build confidence against the time constraints of the exam. Pacing is a difficult skill to master, especially in a high-pressure environment, so **practice is vital**.

Set time expectations for your pace based on how much time is available. For example, if a section has 60 questions and the time limit is 30 minutes, you know you have to average 30 seconds or less per question in order to answer them all. Although 30 seconds is the hard limit, set 25 seconds per question as your goal, so you reserve extra time to spend on harder questions. When you budget extra time for the harder questions, you no longer have any reason to stress when those questions take longer to answer.

Don't let this time expectation distract you from working through the test at a calm, steady pace, but keep it in mind so you don't spend too much time on any one question. Recognize that taking extra time on one question you don't understand may keep you from answering two that you do understand later in the test. If your time limit for a question is up and you're still not sure of the answer, mark it and move on, and come back to it later if the time and the test format allow. If the testing format doesn't allow you to return to earlier questions, just make an educated guess; then put it out of your mind and move on.

On the easier questions, be careful not to rush. It may seem wise to hurry through them so you have more time for the challenging ones, but it's not worth missing one if you know the concept and just didn't take the time to read the question fully. Work efficiently but make sure you understand the question and have looked at all of the answer choices, since more than one may seem right at first.

Even if you're paying attention to the time, you may find yourself a little behind at some point. You should speed up to get back on track, but do so wisely. Don't panic; just take a few seconds less on each question until you're caught up. Don't guess without thinking, but do look through the answer choices and eliminate any you know are wrong. If you can get down to two choices, it is often worthwhile to guess from those. Once you've chosen an answer, move on and don't dwell on any that you skipped or had to hurry through. If a question was taking too long, chances are it was one of the harder ones, so you weren't as likely to get it right anyway.

On the other hand, if you find yourself getting ahead of schedule, it may be beneficial to slow down a little. The more quickly you work, the more likely you are to make a careless mistake that will affect your score. You've budgeted time for each question, so don't be afraid to spend that time. Practice an efficient but careful pace to get the most out of the time you have.

Test-Taking Strategies

This section contains a list of test-taking strategies that you may find helpful as you work through the test. By taking what you know and applying logical thought, you can maximize your chances of answering any question correctly!

It is very important to realize that every question is different and every person is different: no single strategy will work on every question, and no single strategy will work for every person. That's why we've included all of them here, so you can try them out and determine which ones work best for different types of questions and which ones work best for you.

Question Strategies

⊘ READ CAREFULLY

Read the question and the answer choices carefully. Don't miss the question because you misread the terms. You have plenty of time to read each question thoroughly and make sure you understand what is being asked. Yet a happy medium must be attained, so don't waste too much time. You must read carefully and efficiently.

⊘ CONTEXTUAL CLUES

Look for contextual clues. If the question includes a word you are not familiar with, look at the immediate context for some indication of what the word might mean. Contextual clues can often give you all the information you need to decipher the meaning of an unfamiliar word. Even if you can't determine the meaning, you may be able to narrow down the possibilities enough to make a solid guess at the answer to the question.

⊘ PREFIXES

If you're having trouble with a word in the question or answer choices, try dissecting it. Take advantage of every clue that the word might include. Prefixes and suffixes can be a huge help. Usually, they allow you to determine a basic meaning. *Pre-* means before, *post-* means after, *pro-* is positive, *de-* is negative. From prefixes and suffixes, you can get an idea of the general meaning of the word and try to put it into context.

⊘ HEDGE WORDS

Watch out for critical hedge words, such as *likely, may, can, sometimes, often, almost, mostly, usually, generally, rarely,* and *sometimes*. Question writers insert these hedge phrases to cover every possibility. Often an answer choice will be wrong simply because it leaves no room for exception. Be on guard for answer choices that have definitive words such as *exactly* and *always*.

⊘ SWITCHBACK WORDS

Stay alert for *switchbacks*. These are the words and phrases frequently used to alert you to shifts in thought. The most common switchback words are *but, although,* and *however*. Others include *nevertheless, on the other hand, even though, while, in spite of, despite,* and *regardless of*. Switchback words are important to catch because they can change the direction of the question or an answer choice.

7

⊘ Face Value

When in doubt, use common sense. Accept the situation in the problem at face value. Don't read too much into it. These problems will not require you to make wild assumptions. If you have to go beyond creativity and warp time or space in order to have an answer choice fit the question, then you should move on and consider the other answer choices. These are normal problems rooted in reality. The applicable relationship or explanation may not be readily apparent, but it is there for you to figure out. Use your common sense to interpret anything that isn't clear.

Answer Choice Strategies

⊘ Answer Selection

The most thorough way to pick an answer choice is to identify and eliminate wrong answers until only one is left, then confirm it is the correct answer. Sometimes an answer choice may immediately seem right, but be careful. The test writers will usually put more than one reasonable answer choice on each question, so take a second to read all of them and make sure that the other choices are not equally obvious. As long as you have time left, it is better to read every answer choice than to pick the first one that looks right without checking the others.

⊘ Answer Choice Families

An answer choice family consists of two (in rare cases, three) answer choices that are very similar in construction and cannot all be true at the same time. If you see two answer choices that are direct opposites or parallels, one of them is usually the correct answer. For instance, if one answer choice says that quantity x increases and another either says that quantity x decreases (opposite) or says that quantity y increases (parallel), then those answer choices would fall into the same family. An answer choice that doesn't match the construction of the answer choice family is more likely to be incorrect. Most questions will not have answer choice families, but when they do appear, you should be prepared to recognize them.

⊘ Eliminate Answers

Eliminate answer choices as soon as you realize they are wrong, but make sure you consider all possibilities. If you are eliminating answer choices and realize that the last one you are left with is also wrong, don't panic. Start over and consider each choice again. There may be something you missed the first time that you will realize on the second pass.

⊘ Avoid Fact Traps

Don't be distracted by an answer choice that is factually true but doesn't answer the question. You are looking for the choice that answers the question. Stay focused on what the question is asking for so you don't accidentally pick an answer that is true but incorrect. Always go back to the question and make sure the answer choice you've selected actually answers the question and is not merely a true statement.

⊘ Extreme Statements

In general, you should avoid answers that put forth extreme actions as standard practice or proclaim controversial ideas as established fact. An answer choice that states the "process should be used in certain situations, if..." is much more likely to be correct than one that states the "process should be discontinued completely." The first is a calm rational statement and doesn't even make a definitive, uncompromising stance, using a hedge word *if* to provide wiggle room, whereas the second choice is far more extreme.

⊘ Benchmark

As you read through the answer choices and you come across one that seems to answer the question well, mentally select that answer choice. This is not your final answer, but it's the one that will help you evaluate the other answer choices. The one that you selected is your benchmark or standard for judging each of the other answer choices. Every other answer choice must be compared to your benchmark. That choice is correct until proven otherwise by another answer choice beating it. If you find a better answer, then that one becomes your new benchmark. Once you've decided that no other choice answers the question as well as your benchmark, you have your final answer.

⊘ Predict the Answer

Before you even start looking at the answer choices, it is often best to try to predict the answer. When you come up with the answer on your own, it is easier to avoid distractions and traps because you will know exactly what to look for. The right answer choice is unlikely to be word-for-word what you came up with, but it should be a close match. Even if you are confident that you have the right answer, you should still take the time to read each option before moving on.

General Strategies

⊘ Tough Questions

If you are stumped on a problem or it appears too hard or too difficult, don't waste time. Move on! Remember though, if you can quickly check for obviously incorrect answer choices, your chances of guessing correctly are greatly improved. Before you completely give up, at least try to knock out a couple of possible answers. Eliminate what you can and then guess at the remaining answer choices before moving on.

⊘ Check Your Work

Since you will probably not know every term listed and the answer to every question, it is important that you get credit for the ones that you do know. Don't miss any questions through careless mistakes. If at all possible, try to take a second to look back over your answer selection and make sure you've selected the correct answer choice and haven't made a costly careless mistake (such as marking an answer choice that you didn't mean to mark). This quick double check should more than pay for itself in caught mistakes for the time it costs.

⊘ Pace Yourself

It's easy to be overwhelmed when you're looking at a page full of questions; your mind is confused and full of random thoughts, and the clock is ticking down faster than you would like. Calm down and maintain the pace that you have set for yourself. Especially as you get down to the last few minutes of the test, don't let the small numbers on the clock make you panic. As long as you are on track by monitoring your pace, you are guaranteed to have time for each question.

⊘ Don't Rush

It is very easy to make errors when you are in a hurry. Maintaining a fast pace in answering questions is pointless if it makes you miss questions that you would have gotten right otherwise. Test writers like to include distracting information and wrong answers that seem right. Taking a little extra time to avoid careless mistakes can make all the difference in your test score. Find a pace that allows you to be confident in the answers that you select.

⊘ KEEP MOVING

Panicking will not help you pass the test, so do your best to stay calm and keep moving. Taking deep breaths and going through the answer elimination steps you practiced can help to break through a stress barrier and keep your pace.

Final Notes

The combination of a solid foundation of content knowledge and the confidence that comes from practicing your plan for applying that knowledge is the key to maximizing your performance on test day. As your foundation of content knowledge is built up and strengthened, you'll find that the strategies included in this chapter become more and more effective in helping you quickly sift through the distractions and traps of the test to isolate the correct answer.

Now that you're preparing to move forward into the test content chapters of this book, be sure to keep your goal in mind. As you read, think about how you will be able to apply this information on the test. If you've already seen sample questions for the test and you have an idea of the question format and style, try to come up with questions of your own that you can answer based on what you're reading. This will give you valuable practice applying your knowledge in the same ways you can expect to on test day.

Good luck and good studying!

Science

Scientific Investigation and Reasoning

SAFETY PROCEDURES

Everyone working in a lab setting should be careful to follow these rules to protect themselves and others from injury or accidents.

- Students should wear a **lab apron** and **safety goggles**.
- **Loose** or **dangling** clothing and jewelry, necklaces, and earrings should not be worn.
- Those with **long hair** should tie it back.
- Care should always be taken not to **splash chemicals**.
- **Open-toed shoes** such as sandals and flip-flops should not be worn, nor should wrist watches.
- **Glasses** are preferable to contact lenses since the latter carries a risk of chemicals getting caught between the lens and the eye.
- Students should always be **supervised** during an experiment.
- The area where the experiment is taking place and the surrounding floor should be **free of clutter**.
- **Food** and **drink** should also not be allowed in a lab setting.
- **Cords** should not be allowed to **dangle** from work stations.
- There should be no **rough-housing** in the lab.
- **Wash hands** before and after the lab is complete.

SAFETY GLOVES

There are many types of **gloves** available to help protect the skin from cuts, burns, and chemical splashes. There are many considerations to take into account when choosing a glove. For example, gloves that are highly protective may limit grip or accuracy. Some gloves may not offer appropriate protection against a specific chemical. Disposable latex, vinyl, or nitrile gloves are usually appropriate for most circumstances, and offer protection from incidental splashes and contact.

LABORATORY ACCIDENTS

Accidents happen in labs, so it is important to know how to clean up, stay safe, and report the accident to the teacher. Any spills or accidents should be **reported** to the teacher so that the teacher can determine the safest clean-up method. The student should start to wash off a **chemical** spilled on the skin while reporting the incident. Some spills may require removal of contaminated clothing and use of the **safety shower**. Broken glass should be disposed of in a designated container. If someone's clothing catches fire they should walk to the safety shower and use it to extinguish the flames. A fire blanket may be used to smother a **lab fire**. A fire extinguisher, phone, spill neutralizers, and a first aid box are other types of **safety equipment** found in the lab. Students should be familiar with **routes** out of the room and the building in case of fire.

NATURAL RESOURCES, RENEWABLE RESOURCES, NONRENEWABLE RESOURCES, AND COMMODITIES

Natural resources are things provided by nature that have value to humans, such as minerals, energy, timber, fish, wildlife, and the landscape. **Renewable resources** are those that can be replenished, such as wind, solar radiation, tides, and water (with proper conservation and clean-

11

up). Soil is renewable with proper conservation and management techniques, and timber can be replenished with replanting. Living resources such as fish and wildlife can replenish themselves if they are not over-harvested. **Nonrenewable resources** are those that cannot be replenished. These include fossil fuels such as oil and coal and metal ores. These cannot be replaced or reused once they have been burned, although some of their products can be recycled. **Commodities** are natural resources that have to be extracted and purified rather than created, such as mineral ores.

RECYCLING AND PROTECTING THE ENVIRONMENT

When trash is thrown away without separating it out for recycling, it usually goes to a landfill where it cannot be recovered and reused. Metal and plastic do not break down readily, and by sending those to the general trash, those materials are essentially lost. Aluminum cans, like soda cans and canned foods can be recycled and used to make new products down the line. The same can be said of most paper and plastics. Recycling bins are usually next to normal trash cans and have the recycle symbol marked on it. This is usually three arrows pointing at each other in a triangle:

DEFINITION OF SCIENCE

Scientific knowledge is knowledge about the world that we understand by observing and testing. The **scientific process** is how we try to gain scientific knowledge. The steps are to make an initial observation, make a hypothesis, test the hypothesis with an experiment, draw conclusions from the experiment, then start over with new observations.

OBSERVATIONS

An **observation** is something specific you notice about the world or an event. For instance, a very obvious event that takes place is if we leave milk out on the counter overnight, the milk will go bad. We observe this event by using our five senses: sight, taste, smell, touch, and sound. When milk goes bad, there are several ways it changes.

HYPOTHESIS

The next step of the scientific process is to make an educated guess about what might happen in a certain event. This is also known as a **hypothesis**. A hypothesis about milk might be that if I keep milk above a certain temperature for a long time, it will go bad. Hypotheses need to be specific and testable so we can decide if it is true or false.

EXPERIMENT

The step after making a hypothesis is to check if it is true by testing it with an **experiment**. Experiments need to be a controlled, specific situation that tells us if our educated guess was correct. Experiments need to ask questions about **facts**, rather than **opinions**. Usually, the more specific the experiment, the clearer the answer will be. For instance, if I test my hypothesis by putting milk outside overnight, but do not set a timer, then I can get an answer, but I will not be able to record how time affected the experiment. Similarly, if the milk is outside and the temperature

12

changes overnight, I will not be able to learn much about what effect the temperature had on the milk.

VARIABLES

These two aspects of the experiment are examples of variables. **Variables** are parts of the experiment that can change. Some variables are controlled, while others are aspects that we observe. For instance, we cannot control time, but we can observe the milk over time by checking it every half hour. Temperature, on the other hand, can be controlled with technology. We can keep the milk inside the house, where the temperature will always be around 70 degrees, or we can keep it in the refrigerator, where the milk will stay close to 40 degrees. These variables need to be controlled as best as possible to get the most specific results.

REPEATING EXPERIMENTS

Experiments should be **repeated** to see if the same result happens every time. For example, if you can get the same result only three out of ten attempts, then the result is not reliable and the experiment should be changed and tried again. Another example is that if you are testing how milk changes by setting it out, try changing the temperature each time to see if the same result happens at different temperatures.

REFLECT

After an experiment is complete, the scientist needs to **reflect** on what happened by asking questions:

- Did the experiment answer the question?
- Was the hypothesis true or false?
- Did repeated attempts produce the same results?
- Is there anything I should change for future attempts?
- What did I learn?
- What questions can I ask now that I have learned something?

REPEAT THE PROCESS

After the experiment and reflection is over, the scientist hopefully learned something and can ask new questions. These questions should be more specific, or the experiment should be improved to get better answers.

OBSERVED AND MEASURED DATA

Data can be either measurable or observable. **Observable data** is often referred to as **qualitative data**, because it describes specific **qualities** of something being observed. An example of this is color or smell. It is very difficult to find numbers to describe a color or smell, but it is not hard to describe that a liquid changed from red to blue. **Measurable data** is also known as **quantitative data** because it refers to the quantity or amount of something. A good example of quantitative data is weight. Any time someone steps on a scale to know how much they weigh, they are looking at quantitative data. Both types of data are important to keep track of and record.

METRIC SYSTEM

The **metric system** is the accepted standard of measurement in the scientific community. **Standardization** is helpful because it allows the results of experiments to be compared and reproduced without the need to laboriously convert measurements. Metric system uses similar conversions between all types of measurement, including length, mass, volume, time, and temperature.

ENGLISH AND METRIC (SCIENTIFIC) UNITS OF MEASUREMENT

The English system commonly used in the United States is not based on consistent smaller units. Thus, 12 inches equal 1 foot, 3 feet equal 1 yard, and 5,280 feet equal 1 mile. The metric system used in science and most countries of the world is based on units of 10. Therefore, 1000 millimeters and 100 centimeters equal 1 meter, and 1,000 meters equal a kilometer. The same pattern is true for the other units of measurement in the two systems. The following table shows the different units.

Unit	English System	Metric System
length	inch, foot, mile	centimeter, meter, kilometer
mass, weight	net weight ounce, pound	gram, kilogram, newton
volume	fluid ounce, pint, quart	milliliter, liter
temperature	Fahrenheit degree	Celsius degree

FAHRENHEIT AND CELSIUS TEMPERATURE SCALES

In the Fahrenheit scale the point where water freezes and ice melts is set at 32°, and the point where water boils and water vapor condenses is 212°. That means a difference of 180° between the freezing and boiling points of water. In the Celsius scale, the freezing/melting point is set at 0° and the boiling/condensation point at 100°, making this scale much easier to use.

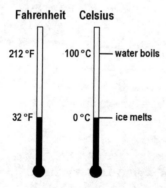

BASIC UNITS OF MEASUREMENT

Using the **metric system** is generally accepted as the preferred method for taking measurements. Having a **universal standard** allows individuals to interpret measurements more easily, regardless of where they are located. The basic units of measurement are: the **meter**, which measures length; the **liter**, which measures volume; and the **gram**, which measures mass. The metric system starts with a base unit and increases or decreases in units of 10. The prefix and the base unit combined are used to indicate an amount. For example, deka- is 10 times the base unit. A dekameter is 10 meters; a dekaliter is 10 liters; and a dekagram is 10 grams. The prefix hecto- refers to 100 times the base amount; kilo- is 1,000 times the base amount. The prefixes that indicate a fraction of the base unit are deci-, which is 1/10 of the base unit; centi-, which is 1/100 of the base unit; and milli-, which is 1/1000 of the base unit.

14

COMMON PREFIXES

The prefixes for **multiples** are as follows:

- **deka** (da), 10 (deka is the American spelling, but deca is also used)
- **hecto** (h), 100
- **kilo** (k), 1000
- **mega** (M), 100,000

The prefixes for **subdivisions** are as follows:

- **deci** (d), 1/10
- **centi** (c), 1/100
- **milli** (m), 1/1000
- **micro** (µ), 1/100,000

VENN DIAGRAMS

One helpful way of sorting out information when comparing two things is a **venn diagram.** This tool is essentially just two circles that overlap, and it is used to display what aspects of one thing are similar or different from another thing. In the following diagram, notice how fish and frogs are similar in some ways, but different in others.

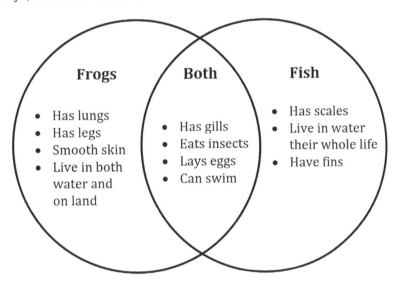

FREQUENCY TABLES

Frequency tables show how frequently each unique value appears in a set. A **relative frequency table** is one that shows the proportions of each unique value compared to the entire set. Relative frequencies are given as percentages; however, the total percent for a relative frequency table will not necessarily equal 100 percent due to rounding. An example of a frequency table with relative frequencies is below.

Favorite Color	Frequency	Relative Frequency
Blue	4	13%
Red	7	22%
Green	3	9%
Purple	6	19%
Cyan	12	38%

CIRCLE GRAPHS

Circle graphs, also known as *pie charts*, provide a visual depiction of the relationship of each type of data compared to the whole set of data. The circle graph is divided into sections by drawing radii to create central angles whose percentage of the circle is equal to the individual data's percentage of the whole set. Each 1% of data is equal to 3.6° in the circle graph. Therefore, data represented by a 90° section of the circle graph makes up 25% of the whole. When complete, a circle graph often looks like a pie cut into uneven wedges. The pie chart below shows the data from the frequency table referenced earlier where people were asked their favorite color.

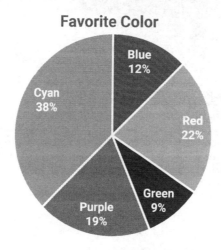

PICTOGRAPHS

A **pictograph** is a graph, generally in the horizontal orientation, that uses pictures or symbols to represent the data. Each pictograph must have a key that defines the picture or symbol and gives the quantity each picture or symbol represents. Pictures or symbols on a pictograph are not always shown as whole elements. In this case, the fraction of the picture or symbol shown represents the same fraction of the quantity a whole picture or symbol stands for. For example, a row with $3\frac{1}{2}$ ears of corn, where each ear of corn represents 100 stalks of corn in a field, would equal $3\frac{1}{2} \times 100 = 350$ stalks of corn in the field.

LINE GRAPHS

Line graphs have one or more lines of varying styles (solid or broken) to show the different values for a set of data. The individual data are represented as ordered pairs, much like on a Cartesian plane. In this case, the x- and y-axes are defined in terms of their units, such as dollars or time. The individual plotted points are joined by line segments to show whether the value of the data is increasing (line sloping upward), decreasing (line sloping downward), or staying the same (horizontal line). Multiple sets of data can be graphed on the same line graph to give an easy visual comparison. An example of this would be graphing achievement test scores for different groups of students over the same time period to see which group had the greatest increase or decrease in performance from year to year (as shown below).

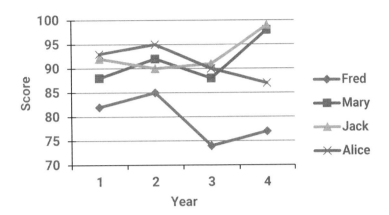

Review Video: Line Graphs
Visit mometrix.com/academy and enter code: 480147

LINE PLOTS

A **line plot**, also known as a *dot plot,* has plotted points that are not connected by line segments. In this graph, the horizontal axis lists the different possible values for the data, and the vertical axis lists the number of times the individual value occurs. A single dot is graphed for each value to show the number of times it occurs. This graph is more closely related to a bar graph than a line graph. Do not connect the dots in a line plot or it will misrepresent the data.

Review Video: Line Plot
Visit mometrix.com/academy and enter code: 754610

STEM AND LEAF PLOTS

A **stem and leaf plot** is useful for depicting groups of data that fall into a range of values. Each piece of data is separated into two parts: the first, or left, part is called the stem; the second, or right, part is called the leaf. Each stem is listed in a column from smallest to largest. Each leaf that has the common stem is listed in that stem's row from smallest to largest. For example, in a set of two-digit numbers, the digit in the tens place is the stem, and the digit in the ones place is the leaf. With a stem and leaf plot, you can easily see which subset of numbers (10s, 20s, 30s, etc.) is the largest. This information is also readily available by looking at a histogram, but a stem and leaf plot also allows you to look closer and see exactly which values fall in that range. Using all of the test scores from above, we can assemble a stem and leaf plot like the one below.

Test Scores

7	4 8
8	2 5 7 8 8
9	0 0 1 2 2 3 5 8 9

BAR GRAPHS

A **bar graph** is one of the few graphs that can be drawn correctly in two different configurations – both horizontally and vertically. A bar graph is similar to a line plot in the way the data is organized on the graph. Both axes must have their categories defined for the graph to be useful. Rather than placing a single dot to mark the point of the data's value, a bar, or thick line, is drawn from zero to the exact value of the data, whether it is a number, percentage, or other numerical value. Longer bar lengths correspond to greater data values. To read a bar graph, read the labels for the axes to find the units being reported. Then, look where the bars end in relation to the scale given on the corresponding axis and determine the associated value.

The bar chart below represents the responses from our favorite-color survey.

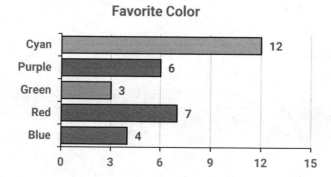

SCIENTIFIC MODELS

Scientists often create **models** to help express and understand scientific ideas. A model is a representation of an idea that is used to experience something that cannot be experienced directly. For instance, we cannot see and experience evaporation directly, but we can easily draw out the process of evaporation, condensation, and precipitation. Having a drawing helps us to understand the concept since we cannot experience it directly. Models can be three-dimensional, such as something you can hold, or they can be simple diagrams demonstrating a process. For instance, a planetarium is a large model that helps someone see the size of planets and stars and how they interact. More typical models in the classroom include baking soda and vinegar volcanoes, solar system mobiles, or molecules made from foam and straws. Other models can include a diagram showing the water cycle.

LIMITATIONS OF MODELS

Using models can be very helpful for experiencing a scientific process that normally couldn't be observed directly, but they are naturally limited. Models are usually used to express a very large thing in a small way, such as a volcano or the planet earth in a way that a human can look at it and touch it. Models are also often used to express very small things or invisible things in a more observable way. Changing the size or the materials used to express something heavily limits how effective a model is. For instance, if a model on the water cycle used cotton balls to show clouds, it impairs our understanding of clouds. Clouds are not made of dry, solid cotton, but are made up of vapor filled with water. Volcanos made from clay and that use baking soda and vinegar do not demonstrate the extreme heat or mass of volcanic materials. Similarly, a mobile of the solar system cannot express how extremely large the sun and planets are. When using a model to understand a concept, the observer needs to be aware that they are probably only getting a clear picture of one side of the concept, and not understanding it fully.

TOOLS FOR MEASURING AND OBSERVATION

Purpose	Tool
Measuring Length	Rulers, meter sticks
Measuring Weight or Mass	Spring scales, pan balances
Measuring Volume	Beakers, graduated cylinders
Measuring Time	Timers, clocks
Measuring Temperature	Thermometer
Recording Information	Journals, notebooks
Observing Animals and Plants	Terrariums, aquariums, collecting nets
Observing Weather	Rain Gauges, wind vanes,
Models for Understanding Concepts	Sun-Earth-Moon System Models, volcano models, water cycle models
Visual Observation	cameras, hand lenses, microscopes

SCIENCE CAREERS

Almost all fields require people who think like scientists or use science directly.

- **Meteorologists** – study the atmosphere to predict weather.
- **Engineers** – use physics and chemistry to design complicated technology and processes.
- **Doctors** – use biology to learn how the body and disease works.
- **Astronomers** – use physics and space science to study the Earth and the universe and travel into space.

CONTRIBUTIONS OF SCIENTISTS

- **Sir Francis Bacon** – contributed many ideas that helped develop the modern scientific method.
- **Gallileo Galilei**– one of the first people to use a telescope and contributed ideas about how gravity works. He also contributed the idea that the Earth revolved around the Sun, and not the other way around.
- **Leonardo da Vinci** – known for his contributions to art and to science, he was an avid inventor, designing a submarine, an armored tank, and several aircraft far before any of which were actually built.
- **Sir Isaac Newton** – best known for his contributions to physics. He described the principals of inertia and friction.
- **Louis Pasteur** – discovered bacteria and invented the process of pasteurization and developed some of the first vaccines.
- **Thomas Edison** – invented many distinct devices, including the phonograph, improved upon the telephone, the lightbulb, and the kinetoscope, an early form of movie projector.
- **Albert Einstein** – studied theoretical physics with the use of mathematics and is particularly famous for his theory of relativity

19

Physical Science

PROPERTIES OF MATTER

Matter is anything that takes up space and has weight. Even air has weight and takes up space. All types of matter have different properties that can be observed or measured. There are many properties of matter, including temperature, mass, magnetism, and the ability to sink or float.

TEMPERATURE

Temperature is a property that tells how hot or cold a thing is. **Temperature** also demonstrates how much **thermal energy** is in a thing. When an object is cold, it has very little thermal energy. For many substances, being hot makes the substance expand, while being cold makes it shrink. Temperature also tends to transfer from one object to another. For instance, when a cup is filled with ice and water, the ice and water exchange energy until they are the same temperature. The ice and water reach the same temperature eventually, usually resulting in the ice melting.

MASS AND WEIGHT

Mass is a measure of how much **matter** is in an object. **Mass** is usually measured by placing an object on a scale. The terms mass and weight are often used interchangeably, but they actually have different definitions. Mass is always the same for a specific object, but **weight** depends on other factors. For instance, 1,000 lb. car always has the same mass, but it would weigh different amounts depending on if the car were on Earth or on Mars, which has much lower gravity.

VOLUME AND DENSITY

Volume is a measure of the **size** of an object or how much space an object takes up. Volume affects several other factors like density. Density is the amount of **mass** (amount of matter) in a certain **volume**. The more matter there is, the more mass an object has. **Density** takes into account both the mass and volume of an object. For instance, an inflated balloon has very little mass in it, but it is fairly large. A watermelon is about the same size, but has much more mass in it, so the watermelon is denser than the balloon. Density is the reason things float or sink. One example is oil and water. Oil is usually thicker than water, but it is actually less dense. If you put oil and water in a cup, you can see that the oil always **floats** to the top. Another way of thinking about it is that the water is actually **sinking** in the oil.

DENSITY OF WATER AND ICE

Most solids have more matter than the same volume of their liquids. This means that they are denser and sink in their own liquid. However, water is different. The molecules in ice are farther apart than they are in liquid water. That means that ice has less matter in it than the same volume of liquid water. Therefore, ice is less dense and floats in water.

MAGNETISM

Magnetism is a property that some rocks or metals can possess. **Magnetism** is a force that can push or pull on other magnetic materials. Magnets always have two poles, which attract the opposite pole and repel the same pole. Usually, the poles on a magnet are identified as being North or South, because the Earth's North and South Poles are actually magnetic as well. This is the reason that compasses work. The small needle in a compass is attracted to the Earth's poles and points in that direction. Many types of technology use magnetism, including electronics, motors, credit cards, and others.

PHYSICAL CHANGES

Physical changes are those that do not affect the chemical properties of a substance. Changes in state are **physical changes**. For example, a liquid can freeze into a solid or boil into a gas without changing the chemical nature of the substance. It is all still the same substance. Ice, steam, and liquid water are all still water, H_2O. Physical properties include such features as shape, texture, size, volume, mass, and density. Cutting, melting, dissolving, mixing, breaking, and crushing are all types of physical changes.

CHEMICAL CHANGES

Chemical changes occur when chemical bonds are broken and new ones are formed. The original substances are **transformed** into different substances. If vinegar and baking soda are mixed together, a lot of bubbles (carbon dioxide) and water will form. Burning wood in a fireplace is another type of chemical change. The carbon in the wood reacts with oxygen in the air to make ash, carbon dioxide, smoke and energy that we feel as heat and see as light.

Examples of chemical changes include the following:

- (a) The temperature of a system changes without any heating or cooling.
- (b) The formation of a gas (bubbles).
- (c) The formation of a precipitate (solid) when two liquids are mixed.
- (d) A liquid changes color.

A **chemical change** occurs when two or more substances come together and interact in such a way that they become completely new substances. For example, two hydrogen atoms and one oxygen atom combine to make a new compound—a water molecule, H_2O. Likewise, two oxygen atoms and one carbon atom combine to make one molecule of carbon dioxide—CO_2. The two substances that combine are called **reactants,** and the new compound that emerges is the **product**. Chemical reactions (changes) can be much more complicated than this.

STATES OF MATTER

The three states of matter are *solids*, *liquids*, and *gases*. In a **solid** the *atoms* or *molecules* of a substance are close together and locked into place. A solid has a definite shape and volume. In a liquid the atoms or molecules are farther apart. A **liquid** flows and takes the shape of its container. In a **gas** the atoms or molecules are very far apart and have a lot of energy. They will fly completely way if not held inside a container like a balloon or a closed bottle. The state of matter that a substance takes on depends mainly on temperature and pressure. For instance, candle wax is

21

usually a solid in normal temperatures on Earth, but if it heats up, it easily melts. Paper, on the other hand, does not melt, but burns and turns directly into a gas.

Solid	Liquid	Gas
Have a definite shape and size. Usually denser than liquids and gases of the same material.	Have a definite size, but do not have a definite shape.	Does not have a definite size or shape, but matches its container.
• Rocks • Ice Cream • Pencils • Apples	• Milk • Water • Juice • Rain	• Steam • Fire • Helium • Fog

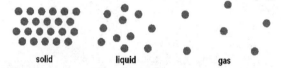

PHASE STATES OF WATER

Water has three states of matter: ice, liquid water, and water vapor. Water freezes at 32 degrees Fahrenheit, where ice crystals form and the substance becomes a solid.

- **Ice** - Water crystalizes when it freezes, which means that it actually expands when it freezes, making it less dense than liquid water. This is uncommon because solids are usually the most dense form of a substance because the atoms are more tightly compressed. That is why ice actually floats in liquid water, rather than sinks.
- **Water Vapor** – Water exists in gas form as it evaporates or boils. Water vapor exists in the air and is often referred to as humidity. There is always some moisture in the air, though as the temperatures drop or pressure changes, it will condense and become liquid water again. Just like all other gas forms, water vapor spreads out in its container and flows much like a liquid.
- **Liquid Water** – Liquid water is the most common form on Earth. Water is needed for life and makes up most of the matter in a human body. Liquid water follows all of the typical rules for liquids, including taking the shape of its container, but has a constant mass and volume.

EXAMPLE

On a cold day breathe into a glass jar with a screw-on lid until droplets of water from your breath condense (change from a gas to a liquid) onto the inside of the jar. Then screw the lid down and put the jar in a warm window or other warm spot. As the air inside the jar warms, the water droplets will evaporate into an invisible gas and will disappear. Now cool the jar down again (perhaps outside in the cold) and watch as the water droplets form again.

MIXTURES

A **mixture** is made of two or more substances that are combined There are two types of mixtures: homogeneous and heterogeneous. **Homogeneous** means that the mixture's ingredients are perfectly distributed and are the same throughout. An example of a homogenous mixture is salt water. If you mix salt into water so well that it dissolves, the salt becomes evenly distributed into the water and cannot normally be separated. **Heterogeneous** means that the mixture's composition and properties are not uniform throughout. Examples of heterogenous mixtures

22

include cereal in milk, ice in a drink, and sand in water. Consider that if you mix sand in water and stir it up, the sand settles to the bottom. If the parts being mixed together do not stay perfectly mixed, then the mixture is heterogenous. Mixtures do not have to be a particular state of matter; they can be solids, liquids, or gases. For instance, if you consider a chocolate chip cookie, the cookie is a mixture of the cookie bread and chocolate chips. The bread itself is made of flour, sugar, and eggs, which mix together to make a homogenous mixture. Once the chocolate chips are added in, the mixture is heterogenous, because the chocolate chips do not distribute perfectly throughout the mixture.

SOLUTIONS

The term **solution** refers to a mixture of two or more substances that are completely dissolved. Mixtures can usually be sorted or filtered to separate out the different ingredients, but this is not possible with a solution. For instance, coffee is made by mixing ground coffee beans into water, and then is filtered to separate the coffee grounds. Very small particles of the coffee grounds dissolve into the water so well that they cannot be filtered out, which is why the coffee beverage remains brown, even after being filtered. Another example is salt being mixed with water. Once the salt is stirred into water, the grains dissolve completely and won't settle out and cannot be filtered out. This is called a solution.

TYPES OF ENERGY

There are many different **types of energy** that exist. These include mechanical, sound, magnetic, electrical, light, heat, and chemical. From the first law of thermodynamics, we know that energy cannot be **created** or **destroyed**, but it may be **converted** from one form to another. This does not mean that all forms of energy are useful. Indeed, the second law states that net useful energy decreases in every process that takes place. Most often this occurs when other forms of energy are converted to heat through means such as friction. In these cases, the heat is quickly absorbed into the surroundings and becomes unusable.

ENERGY CONVERSION

There are many examples of energy conversion, such as in an automobile. The **chemical energy** in the gasoline is converted to **mechanical energy** in the engine. Subsequently, this mechanical energy is converted to **kinetic energy** as the car moves. Additionally, the mechanical energy is converted to **electrical energy** to power the radio, headlights, air conditioner, and other devices. In the radio, electrical energy is converted to **sound energy**. In the headlights, it is converted to **heat** and **light energy**. In the air conditioner, it does work to remove heat energy from the car's interior. It is important to remember that, in all of these processes, a portion of the energy is lost from its intended purpose.

EXAMPLES OF ENERGY

- Candles convert chemical energy to light and heat as they burn.
- Hydro-electric dams and wind turbines convert mechanical energy into electricity.
- The sun uses nuclear energy to create heat and light.
- Light bulbs convert electrical energy into light and heat.
- Speakers convert electricity into sound energy.

CONDUCTORS AND INSULATORS

The terms conductor and insulator refer to how easily a material transfers energy to and from another material. Usually, this refers to **thermal** and **electrical** energy. A **conductor** is a material that easily transfers the energy, whereas an **insulator** does not easily transfer energy. Most materials that conduct heat well also conduct electricity well, and vice-versa. One example of a good conductor is copper wire. Copper wire is used in many electrical applications because it conducts electricity well. Most metals, like copper, also conduct heat well and are used in cooking because they heat up quickly and transfer the energy to the food that is being cooked. Examples of insulators include plastic, wood, and air.

CONDUCTORS AND INSULATORS USED TOGETHER

Insulators and conductors are often used together for better effect. For instance, the handle on a frying pan is usually made of silicone or plastic because it does not conduct heat well, whereas the rest of the pan is metal, which does conduct heat. The insulating properties of the plastic handle protect the cook's hand from being burned, while the metal parts of the pan help to cook the food. Insulators are also often used alongside conductors in electrical parts to help direct the flow of electricity and protect from shocks and fires. For instance, most outlets have a mixture of plastic parts and metal parts. The cover and the box that holds the outlet in the wall are usually plastic, and the wiring is covered with plastic to prevent shocks and fires, but the inside parts are usually made of copper, which help the electrical energy flow freely inside.

EXAMPLES OF CONDUCTORS AND INSULATORS

	Conductors	Insulators
Thermal	Aluminum, Copper, Silver, Diamonds	Plastic, Wood, Water, Air
Electrical	Gold, Steel, Copper, Water,	Rubber, Plastic, Glass, Rock, Wood, Air, Diamond

HEAT TRANSFER

Heat is a type of energy. Heat transfers from the hot object to the cold object through the three forms of heat transfer: conduction, convection, and radiation.

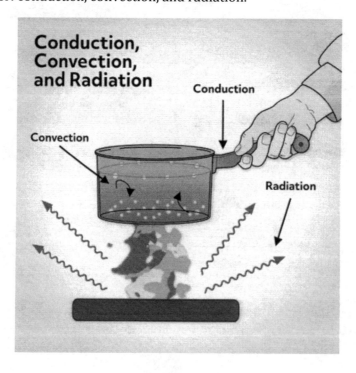

- **Conduction** is the transfer of heat by physical contact. When you touch a hot pot, the pot transfers heat to your hand by conduction.
- **Convection** is the transfer of heat by the movement of fluids. When you put your hand in steam, the steam transfers heat to your hand by convection.
- **Radiation** is the transfer of heat by electromagnetic waves. When you put your hand near a campfire, the fire heats your hand by radiation.

> **Review Video: <u>Heat Transfer</u>**
> Visit mometrix.com/academy and enter code: 451646

ELECTRICAL ENERGY AND CIRCUITS

Electrical energy is the energy of small particles called **electrons** moving from one material to another. All matter has electrons, but some materials allow for their electrons to move more freely, which is why some materials are conductive and others are not. Just like with magnets, electricity can have a positive, negative, or neutral charge. Also like with magnets, **opposite charges attract**, whereas same charges repel each other, which is why clothes that are charged with static electricity cling to each other. Lightning is another good example of an electrical charge in nature. Lightning is made by friction between the air and the ground, which causes the ground to become positively charged and the clouds become negatively charged. These charges want to balance out, so when the charges become strong enough, they snap back together suddenly, creating a lightning bolt and causing the charges to neutralize.

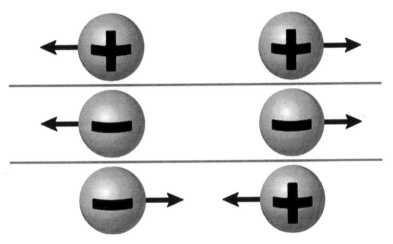

CIRCUITS

Electricity does not flow on its own; there needs to be both an imbalance of negative and positive charges and there needs to be a path for the electrons to **flow** through. This path is called a **circuit**, and it is made of a conductive material, such as wire, that completes a full circle. A circuit also needs to have a **power source**, such as a battery, that pushes the electrical imbalance. When a circuit is complete, electrical energy will flow from positive to negative. The flow of electricity through a circuit is called a **current**. Current can flow through other objects, such as a light bulb, to use the energy without interrupting the circuit.

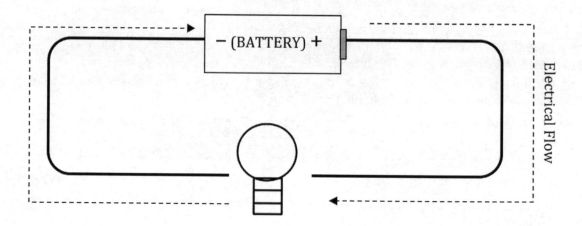

PARTS IN A CIRCUIT

One of the most common parts in a circuit is a switch. To work, a circuit must have a continuous path for the electrical energy to flow through. A switch is simply a device that physically cuts the circuit so that the energy cannot flow. When the circuit is cut, there is no path for the energy to flow. Other common parts in circuits allow the current to flow through them, converting the energy into other forms. These objects are called **load objects** or **resistors**, and they include light bulbs and motors. Light bulbs convert the electrical energy into light, while motors convert the electrical energy into mechanical energy.

GRAVITY

Gravity is a force that exists between all objects with matter. **Gravity** is a pulling force between objects, meaning that the forces on the objects point toward the opposite object. Gravity as we experience it is the force that the Earth exerts on objects, pulling them downward toward the center of the Earth. When Newton's third law is applied to gravity, the force pairs from gravity are shown to be equal in magnitude and opposite in direction.

Technically, all matter pulls other matter. The more massive the object, the more it pulls. The Earth is seen as our center of gravity because it is the most massive object nearby. Gravity is also reason that the Earth and other planets revolve around the Sun. The Sun is so massive that the Earth and all of the other bodies within the solar system are drawn to it and revolve around it as a result.

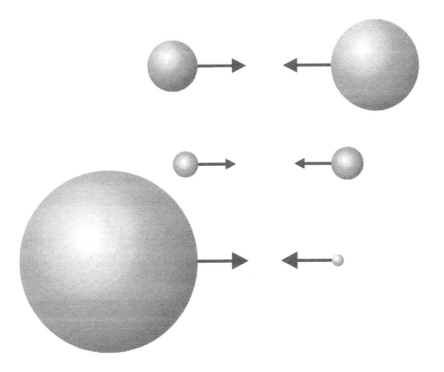

FRICTION

Friction is a resistance to motion between contacting surfaces. In order to illustrate the concept of friction, let us imagine a book resting on a table. As it sits, the force of its weight is equal to and opposite of the normal force. If, however, we were to exert a force on the book, attempting to push it to one side, a frictional force would arise, equal and opposite to our force. This kind of frictional force is known as static frictional force.

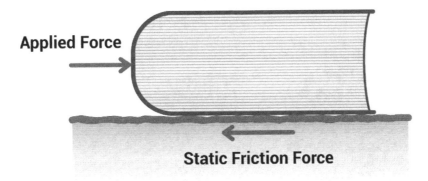

Applied Force

Static Friction Force

As we increase our force on the book, however, we will eventually cause it to accelerate in the direction of our force. At this point, the frictional force opposing us will be known as kinetic friction. For many combinations of surfaces, the magnitude of the kinetic frictional force is lower than that of the static frictional force, and consequently, the amount of force needed to maintain the movement of the book will be less than that needed to initiate the movement.

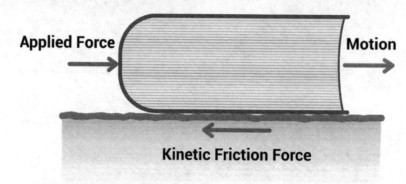

MAGNETISM

Magnetism is an **attraction** between opposite poles of **magnetic materials** and a **repulsion** between similar poles of magnetic materials. Magnetism can be natural or induced with the use of electric currents. Magnets almost always exist with two polar sides: north and south. A magnetic force exists between two poles on objects. Different poles attract each other. Like poles repel each other.

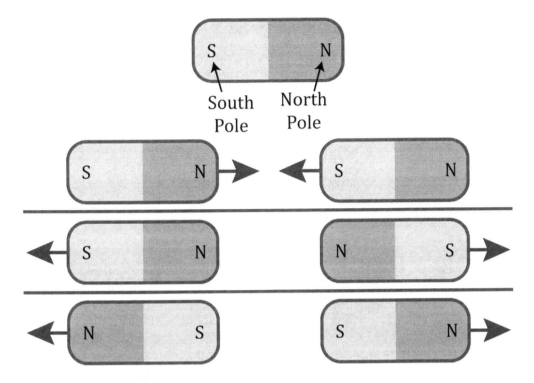

Earth and Space Science

ROCK CYCLE

The **rock cycle** is the process whereby the materials that make up the Earth transition through the three types of rock: igneous, sedimentary, and metamorphic. Rocks, like all matter, cannot be created or destroyed; rather, they undergo a series of changes and adopt different forms through the functions of the rock cycle. Plate tectonics and the water cycle are the driving forces behind the rock cycle; they force rocks and minerals out of equilibrium and force them to adjust to different external conditions. Viewed in a generalized, cyclical fashion, the rock cycle operates as follows: rocks beneath Earth's surface melt into magma. This **magma** either erupts through volcanoes or remains inside the Earth. Regardless, the magma cools, forming igneous rocks. On the surface, these rocks experience **weathering** and **erosion**, which break them down and distribute the fragments across the surface. These fragments form layers and eventually become **sedimentary rocks**. Sedimentary rocks are then either transformed to **metamorphic rocks** (which will become magma inside the Earth) or melted down into magma.

ROCK FORMATION

Igneous Rocks: Igneous rocks can be formed from sedimentary rocks, metamorphic rocks, or other igneous rocks. Rocks that are pushed under the Earth's surface (usually due to plate subduction) are exposed to high mantle temperatures, which cause the rocks to melt into magma. The magma then rises to the surface through volcanic processes. The lower atmospheric temperature causes the magma to cool, forming grainy, extrusive igneous rocks. The creation of extrusive, or volcanic, rocks is quite rapid. The cooling process can occur so rapidly that crystals do not form; in this case, the result is a glass, such as obsidian. It is also possible for magma to cool down inside the Earth's interior; this type of igneous rock is called intrusive. Intrusive, or plutonic, rocks cool more slowly, resulting in a coarse-grained texture.

Sedimentary Rocks: Sedimentary rocks are formed when rocks at the Earth's surface experience weathering and erosion, which break them down and distribute the fragments across the surface. Fragmented material (small pieces of rock, organic debris, and the chemical products of mineral sublimation) is deposited and accumulates in layers, with top layers burying the materials beneath. The pressure exerted by the topmost layers causes the lower layers to compact, creating solid sedimentary rock in a process called lithification.

Metamorphic Rocks: Metamorphic rocks are igneous or sedimentary rocks that have "morphed" into another kind of rock. In metamorphism, high temperatures and levels of pressure change preexisting rocks physically and/or chemically, which produces different species of rocks. In the rock cycle, this process generally occurs in materials that have been thrust back into the Earth's mantle by plate subduction. Regional metamorphism refers to a large band of metamorphic activity; this often occurs near areas of high orogenic (mountain-building) activity. Contact metamorphism refers to metamorphism that occurs when "country rock" (that is, rock native to an area) comes into contact with high-heat igneous intrusions (magma).

ROLE OF WATER

Water plays an important role in the rock cycle through its roles in **erosion** and **weathering**: it wears down rocks; it contributes to the dissolution of rocks and minerals as acidic soil water; and it carries ions and rock fragments (sediments) to basins where they will be compressed into **sedimentary rock**. Water also plays a role in the **metamorphic processes** that occur underwater in newly-formed igneous rock at mid-ocean ridges. The presence of water (and other volatiles) is a vital component in the melting of rocky crust into magma above subduction zones.

> **Review Video: Igneous, Sedimentary, and Metamorphic Rocks**
> Visit mometrix.com/academy and enter code: 689294

SOILS

Soils are formed when rock is broken down into smaller and smaller fragments by physical, chemical, and biological processes. This is called **weathering**. *Physical processes* include **erosion** and **transportation** by water and wind, freezing and thawing, and slumping due to gravity. *Chemical changes* alter the original substances present in rocks and early-stage soils. *Biological processes* include burrowing by animals like earthworms and rodents and penetration by plant roots. As plants and animals die and **decay**, soils become rich in dark organic matter called *humus*.

PROPERTIES OF SOIL

Since soil is a mixture of rock fragments and biological materials, it varies significantly. The composition of soil determines whether it will be good for plant life or not. Several properties of soil can be used to identify its composition, which can be helpful for adjusting it for suitability for plant growth.

- **Texture** refers to the size of the particles, which are classified as sand, silt, or clay, depending on the size and mixture of the particles.
- **Structure** refers to the density and arrangement of the soil particles. Soil can be compacted, making it dense and rock-like or it can be loose and easy to work with when planting.
- **Porosity** refers to how well water flows through the soil. A higher sand content usually allows water to flow through the soil more easily, whereas clay tends to hold onto water.
- **Chemistry** cannot be seen, but can be tested for the actual elements present in a sample of soil.
- **Color** of soil changes based on the types of minerals and organic matter in the soil. Redder soil may indicate that there is oxidized (rusted) iron in the soil, for instance.

NATURAL RESOURCES

The term **natural resources** refers to products and energy that can be harvested from the world and used.

- **Water** is one of the most abundant resources on the earth and is necessary for life.
- **Natural gas** and **oil** exist underground and deep in the ocean and can be used as fuel for machines.

31

- **Trees** can be harvested for wood and paper and other byproducts that are used in daily life.
- **Metals** can be harvested from the ground and are used in many applications, such as building materials and in electronics.
- **Sand** can be used to make glass, soaps, and electronics.
- **Sunlight** and **wind** can be harvested with solar panels and wind turbines to generate electricity.
- **Animal products** are used for food or materials in clothing and some manufacturing processes.

RENEWABLE AND NON-RENEWABLE RESOURCES

Materials and energy on the Earth are classified as either renewable or non-renewable. The term **renewable resources** refers to resources that are not going to run out due to overuse or can be easily reclaimed once used. This includes the sun, wind, and water. Some plants and animals grow so fast that it would be very challenging to run out and cause any form of extinction. **Non-renewable resources** include materials that take a very long time to produce, such as fossil fuels and coal. Once the Earth's population uses these materials up, it is very difficult to obtain or impossible to create more. Because renewable resources do not run out, whereas non-renewable resources do, environmentalists and scientists are always looking for new renewable resources to supply the planet with energy and for ways to reduce consumption of non-renewable resources. This reduction of consumption is known as **conservation**.

WEATHER

Heat energy from the sun warms different parts of the planet in different ways at different times. As warm air rises it expands and cools. This causes moisture to condense as liquid drops or freeze as ice crystals to form clouds. When the water drops or ice crystals become too large to stay aloft, they fall as precipitation. As warm air rises it also leaves a low pressure zone behind. This causes air from high surrounding high pressure zones to rush in as wind.

CLOUDS

Clouds form when water vapor in the atmosphere cools to the point where it condenses out as water droplets or small particles of frozen ice crystals that we can see. Clouds can also form when more moisture is added to the air by evaporation until the air becomes saturated and cannot hold any more water. Then the water vapor will begin to condense into visible droplets.

PRECIPITATION FALLING FROM A CLOUD

When the condensed water droplets or ice crystals forming in the cloud grow in size and become too heavy to stay aloft, they fall as rain, snowflakes, or hail.

LIGHTNING BOLT

Lightning is a huge electric spark that can occur inside a cloud, go from one cloud to another, or go from a cloud to the ground. The turbulent rising air and rising and falling raindrops or ice crystals in a thunderstorm cause differences in electric charge in different parts of the cloud and between the bottom of the cloud and the ground. When the difference in charge is large enough, a lightning bolt will discharge which neutralizes the difference.

THUNDER

As a lightning bolt travels through the air, it pushes the air aside faster than the speed of sound. This produces a shock wave of very hot air that creates a loud sonic boom, which we hear as thunder. If a person can hear thunder, he needs to get indoors quickly as possible since he could be struck by lightning.

We hear thunder later because sound travels much slower than light. Light travels so fast that it is almost instantaneous from one point to another anywhere on Earth. Sound travels much more slowly—about one mile every five seconds or so. Light would travel one mile in only about 5 millionths of a second. Therefore, the distance from a lightning flash can be determined by counting the number of seconds until the thunder it made is heard.

TORNADO

A tornado is a violent rotating column of air that is in contact with both the ground and a cloud. The column is visible because the very low pressure causes water vapor to condense out as visible water droplets. Where the tornado touches the ground it usually stirs up a cloud of dirt and debris like the one in this photo. Tornadoes are the most violent storms on Earth, and the strongest spin at 300 miles per hour.

HURRICANE

A hurricane is a very large tropical storm that forms over the open ocean and produces very strong winds and heavy rains. A tropical storm forms when warm water evaporates and the saturated air

33

rises and forms a column of condensed water vapor. As the wind speed increases the pressure falls even more and a hurricane can be born. Sinking air in the center of the storm produces an eye (arrow) where the weather is quite calm and free of clouds.

MEASURING WEATHER

Weather can be measured by a variety of methods. The simplest include measurement of rainfall, sunshine, pressure, humidity, temperature, and cloudiness with basic instruments such as thermometers, barometers, and rain gauges. However, the use of radar (which involves analysis of microwaves reflecting off of raindrops) and satellite imagery grants meteorologists a look at the big picture of weather across, for example, an entire continent. This helps them understand and make predictions about current and developing weather systems. Infrared (heat-sensing) imaging allows meteorologists to measure the temperature of clouds above ground. Using weather reports gathered from different weather stations spread over an area, meteorologists create synoptic charts. The locations and weather reports of several stations are plotted on a chart; analysis of the pressures reported from each location, as well as rainfall, cloud cover, and so on, can reveal basic weather patterns.

WATER CYCLE

The **water cycle** refers to the circulation of water in the Earth's hydrosphere (below the surface, on the surface, and above the surface of the Earth). This continuous process involves five physical actions.

- **Evaporation** refers to liquid water heating up and changing to into a gas, known as water vapor.
- **Transpiration** is where water inside of plants evaporates directly out of plant leaves.
- **Condensation** refers to the water vapor cooling down and beginning to turn back into a liquid form, causing clouds to form.
- **Precipitation** refers to the rain, snow, hail, or sleet that falls from clouds once the water vapor has condensed enough.

- The **storage** stage of the water cycle refers to the water being stored in the ground, trees, or bodies of water on the earth. Water is either trapped in vegetation (interception) or absorbed into the surface (infiltration). Runoff, caused by gravity, physically moves water downward into oceans or other water bodies.

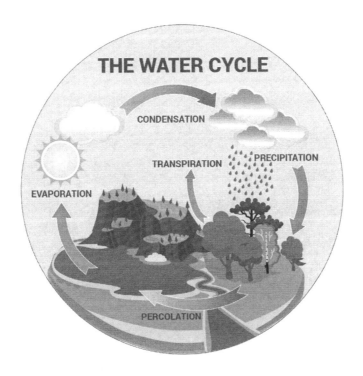

Review Video: <u>Hydrologic Cycle</u>
Visit mometrix.com/academy and enter code: 426578

SUN

The **Sun** is the vital force of life on Earth; it is also the central component of our solar system. It is basically a sphere of extremely hot gases (close to 15 million degrees at the core) held together by gravity. Some of these gaseous molecules are ionized due to the high temperatures. The balance between its gravitational force and the pressure produced by the hot gases is called **hydrostatic equilibrium**. The source of the solar energy that keeps the Sun alive and plays a key role in the perpetuation of life on Earth is located in the Sun's core, where nucleosynthesis produces heat energy and photons. The Sun's atmosphere consists of the photosphere, the surface visible from Earth, the chromosphere, a layer outside of and hotter than the photosphere, the transition zone (the region where temperatures rise between the chromosphere and the corona), and the corona, which is best viewed at x-ray wavelengths. A solar flare is an explosive emission of ionized particles from the Sun's surface.

Review Video: <u>The Sun</u>
Visit mometrix.com/academy and enter code: 699233

EARTH'S ROTATION

The **Earth rotates** west to east about its axis, an imaginary straight line that runs nearly vertically through the center of the planet. This rotation (which takes 23 hours, 56 minutes, and 5 seconds) places each section of the Earth's surface in a position facing the Sun for a period of time, thus creating the alternating periods of light and darkness we experience as **day and night**. This rotation constitutes a sidereal day; it is measured as the amount of time required for a reference star to cross the meridian (an imaginary north-south line above an observer). Each star crosses the meridian once every (sidereal) day. Since the speed at which Earth rotates is not exactly constant, we use the mean solar day (a 24-hour period) in timekeeping rather than the slightly variable sidereal day.

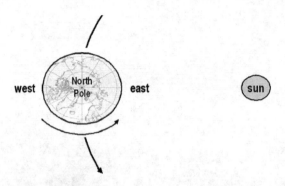

EARTH'S REVOLUTION AROUND THE SUN

Like all celestial objects in our solar system, planet Earth revolves around the Sun. This process takes approximately 365 1/4 days, the period of time that constitutes a calendar year. The path of the orbit of Earth around the Sun is not circular but **elliptical**. Therefore, the distances between the Earth and the Sun at points on either extreme of this counterclockwise orbit are not equal. In other words, the distance between the two objects varies over the course of a year. At **perihelion**, the minimum heliocentric distance, Earth is 147 million kilometers from the Sun. At **aphelion**, the maximum heliocentric distance, Earth is 152 million kilometers from the Sun. This movement of the Earth is responsible for the apparent annual motions of the Sun (in a path referred to as the ecliptic) and other celestial objects visible from Earth's surface.

> **Review Video: <u>Astronomy</u>**
> Visit mometrix.com/academy and enter code: 640556
>
> **Review Video: <u>Solar System</u>**
> Visit mometrix.com/academy and enter code: 273231

PHASES OF THE MOON

As the moon revolves around Earth approximately every 27.3 days, light from the Sun hits it from different angles. This causes the Moon to be in full sunlight (full moon) when Earth is between it and the Sun, complete darkness (new moon) when it is between Earth and the Sun, and all stages in between. When the Moon is half in sunlight and half in shadow it is in the first or last quarter, depending on whether it is heading towards becoming a full moon or a new moon.

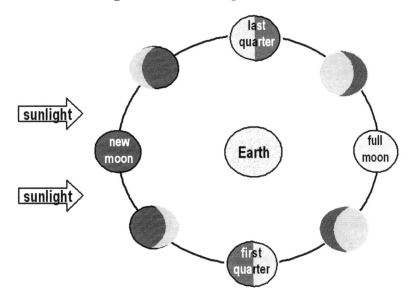

EARTH'S ATMOSPHERE

Earth's gravity is strong enough to attract the molecules of the gases in the atmosphere and keep them in a layer surrounding the planet. The gravity of smaller celestial bodies like Mercury and Earth's moon is not strong enough to do this, and their atmospheres long ago diffused out into space.

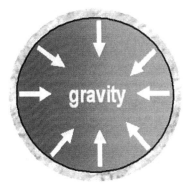

SEASONS

Earth is tilted on its axis as it revolves around the Sun and rotates upon its axis from left to right. That means more sunshine and longer days and shorter nights in the hemisphere facing the Sun. More sunlight means warmer temperatures. In the left-hand picture the Southern Hemisphere is

37

experiencing its summer. Six months later when Earth is on the opposite side of the Sun it is the Northern Hemisphere that is having summer.

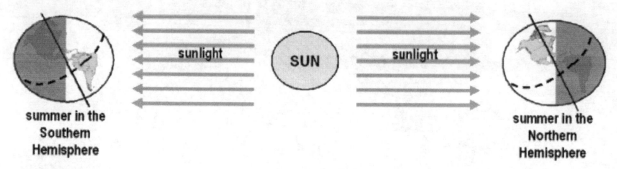

SOLAR SYSTEM

The *solar system* consists of the sun and eight *major planets*. In order from the sun the planets are Mercury, Venus, Earth, Mars, Jupiter, Saturn, Uranus and Neptune. Pluto is no longer considered to be a major planet. Along with 5 other similar sized objects it is now a *minor planet*. Six of the major planets have one or more moons. The solar system also contains countless *meteoroids*, *asteroids*, and *comets*.

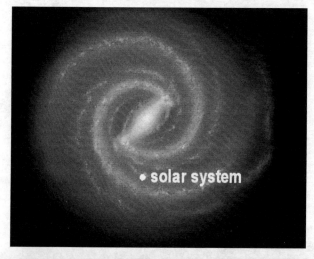

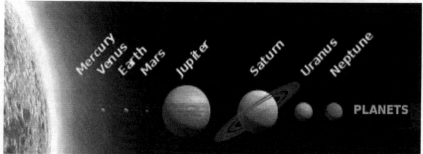

MILKY WAY

On a clear dark moonless night far from city lights a broad white band of stars that stretches across the sky can be seen. This is the Milky Way galaxy, and our sun and the solar system are part of it.

The Milky Way is a huge flat disk containing between 200 billion and 400 billion stars. Because Earth is in that disk, we see it edge on, which is why it appears to us as a broad band of light.

The Milky Way is a flat, disk-shaped spiral galaxy with a central bar-like bulge of stars. It is huge—between 100,000 and 120,000 light-years in diameter. A light-year is a unit of distance, not time. It is the distance light travels in one year, about 6 trillion miles. The Milky Way is between 600 thousand trillion and 700 thousand trillion miles across. Our solar system lies about two thirds of the way out on one of the spiral arms.

COMET

Comets are small icy bodies ranging in size from tens of yards to tens of miles in diameter. They orbit the sun with periods of a few years to hundreds of thousands of years. Halley's comet shown here orbits the sun every 75 to 76 years. As a comet nears the sun a long tail or coma is created as ice and dust are blown off by the intense radiation and the solar wind of charged particles from the sun.

METEOROIDS AND METEORS

A *meteoroid* is a sand- to boulder-sized piece of debris hurtling through the solar system at speeds of between 15 and 45 miles per second. When it enters earth's atmosphere it burns up and leaves a visible fiery trail of gas and debris called a *meteor*. Some meteoroids are large enough that they do not completely burn up, and what remains reaches the ground. These are called *meteorites*. Meteoroids can be small pieces that have broken off of *asteroids*.

Life Science

PRODUCERS, CONSUMERS, AND DECOMPOSERS

Producers are organisms that can make their own food. Most producers are plants. Through photosynthesis plants make sugars that provide energy. Plants only need sunlight, water, and the proper minerals and other nutrients to live, grow, and reproduce themselves. **Consumers** are organisms that eat other organisms. Consumers are animals that eat plants or other animals that eat plants. Decomposers are organisms that feed on decaying plant and animal matter. Since decomposers cannot make their own food they are classified as consumers. Fungi such as mushrooms are **decomposers** that break down the tissues and wood of living or dead plants or the bodies of dead animals.

ENERGY PYRAMID

Energy flow through an ecosystem can be tracked through an energy pyramid. An **energy pyramid** shows how energy is transferred from one trophic level to another. **Producers** always form the base of an energy pyramid, and the consumers form successive levels above the producers. Producers only store about 1% of the solar energy they receive. Then, each successive level only uses about 10% of the energy of the previous level. That means that **primary consumers** use about 10% of the energy used by primary producers, such as grasses and trees. Next, **secondary consumers** use 10% of primary consumers' 10%, or 1% overall. This continues up for as many trophic levels as exist in a particular ecosystem.

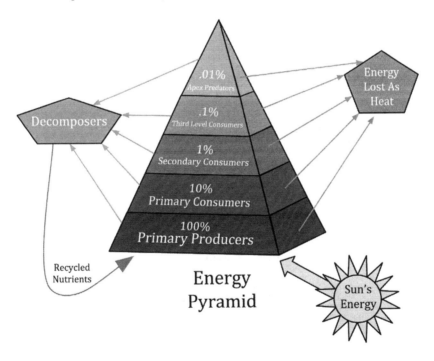

FOOD WEB

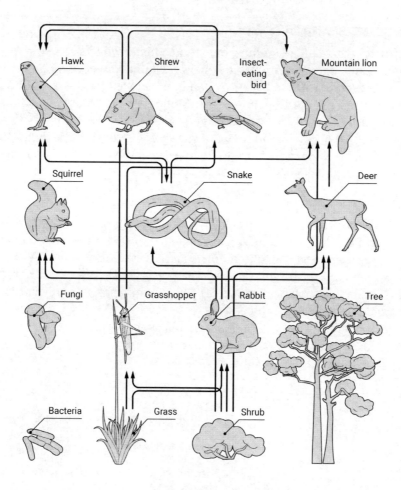

Energy flow through an ecosystem can be illustrated by a **food web**. Energy moves through the food web in the direction of the arrows. In the food web, **producers** such as grass, trees, and shrubs use energy from the sun to produce food through photosynthesis. **Herbivores** or **primary consumers** such as squirrels, grasshoppers, and rabbits obtain energy by eating the producers. **Secondary consumers**, which are carnivores such as snakes and shrews, obtain energy by eating the primary consumers. **Tertiary consumers**, which are carnivores such as hawks and mountain lions, obtain energy by eating the secondary consumers.

> **Review Video: <u>Food Webs</u>**
> Visit mometrix.com/academy and enter code: 853254

INTERDEPENDENCE OF THE FOOD WEB

Because each level of consumer is dependent on the previous level for food, the population of each level affects the other animal groups. For instance, if an ecosystem is made up of only grass, deer, and wolves, the grass are the producers, the deer eat the grass, and the wolves eat the deer. If deer are overhunted one year, the grass is given room to grow more because less of it is consumed, but the wolves will not have enough food, so the population will reduce size. Eventually, because of the abundance of grass and a reduced population of wolves, the deer may then have a surge of population. This example is an over-simplistic example, as there are usually many more producers, consumers, and predators within an ecosystem.

POPULATIONS OF ANIMALS OR PLANTS

A population consists of all of the organisms of a certain kind in a defined area, region, or habitat. It may be all the red foxes in a given national park, all the loblolly pines in Virginia (very hard to count), all the bullfrogs in a certain pond, or even all of the boxelder bugs on a single box elder tree. In the case of rare or endangered species it may be all of the individuals still living in the wild.

Several factors operate to keep animal and plant populations under control. Predation, grazing, disease, competition for limiting resources such as food or nutrients, water, habitat and living space, hunting and breeding territory, and sunlight for plants all play important roles. Even the size of the population can influence factors such as birth rate and severity of disease outbreaks or force individuals to migrate to other less crowded areas.

PLANT SPECIES COMPETING WITH EACH OTHER

Creosote bush is the most widespread shrub in the deserts of the American Southwest where water can be very scarce for long periods. The roots of mature creosote bushes are extremely efficient and absorb all the water in the sandy soil around them. This creates very dry zones around each plant. The seeds of other plants cannot survive long enough to germinate. Therefore, the plants tend to be spaced far apart from each other.

FOOD WEB IN A POND

Sunlight allows green algae to photosynthesize and grow. The algae are fed upon by small animals like water fleas and copepods. In turn, these are eaten by small worms, mosquito larvae and other larval insects. These are then eaten by mosquito fish, which in turn are eaten by larger fishes like bluegills. The bluegills are preyed upon by even larger fishes like bass and by herons, egrets and raccoons (which also eat the bass). Then the animal waste and everything that dies and settles to the bottom is decomposed by bacteria and fungi.

FOOD WEB IN A MEADOW

Sunlight allows grass and other plants to grow. These plants are eaten by a variety of *herbivores* like insects, rodents, and rabbits. Their seeds are consumed by various birds such as sparrows and quail. The insects are eaten by *carnivores*, including other kinds of birds, shrews, and bats. The rodents, rabbits, and some of the birds are then eaten by larger carnivores like weasels and foxes. Also, the quail, mice, rabbits and shrews are eaten by owls at night and by hawks during the day.

ANIMALS OF THE SAME SPECIES COMPETING WITH EACH OTHER

Male elk known as bulls have large antlers, which they shed and regrow each year. Like their smaller deer cousins, bull elk engage in bugling contests and ritual combat (like the photo below) to dominate other males and win all the female (cow) elk in a harem.

Different species of animals often compete for food. The spotted hyena and the African lion shown here compete for prey like zebras and wildebeest. Both hyenas and lions run in groups. A larger pack of hyenas can drive a smaller pride of lions away from prey the lions have killed. However, one lion can easily kill one or more hyenas. They rarely tolerate each other as they seem to be doing below.

ANIMAL MIGRATION

Many animals make a regular two-way, long-distance journey due to seasonal changes affecting the availability of food, weather or rainfall. Birds are especially noted for this, but other animals like bats, some butterflies, moths, and grasshoppers also migrate back and forth between northern winter and southern summer territories. Caribou and wildebeest also make spectacular migrations. The figure at right shows the 14,000-mile migration route of the Swainson's hawk, which spends its summers in western North America and winters in South America.

LEARNED BEHAVIORS IN ANIMALS

Many behaviors in higher animals such as birds and mammals actually have to be learned. Bird songs are usually learned. Male cardinals sing slightly different songs in different areas of the country. They learn these dialects from the adult birds around them. Also, unlike the instinctive migration of spawning salmon, sandhill cranes must be taught the long migration routes they fly between their nesting and winter grounds. Likewise, most predatory mammals must learn how to hunt from their mothers.

FASTEST LAND ANIMAL

The fastest animal on planet Earth is the cheetah. A cheetah can run between 70 and 75 miles per hour for almost two thirds of a mile and can go from a dead stop to 62 miles per hour in three seconds. It stalks its small antelope prey to within a short distance and then chases it down. Since the gazelle being chased in this picture can only run at 50 miles per hour, the faster cheetah has a good chance of running it down.

ANIMALS THAT MOSTLY COME OUT AT NIGHT

Nocturnal animals are active at night and sleep during the day. Nocturnal animals generally have very good senses of hearing and smell, and specially adapted eyes for seeing in the dark. Hunting or foraging for food at night is one way of avoiding competition for those resources from *diurnal* animals that are active during the day. Hawks and owls avoid competing with each other for prey in this way. Nocturnal animals also avoid the intense heat of the day in hot regions like deserts.

HIBERNATION

Hibernation occurs when an animal enters a state of inactivity in which its body temperature drops, and its breathing and metabolism slow down, and it goes into a deep sleep for many days, weeks, or even months. This allows animals to survive long, cold winters when food is scarce. Bears, ground squirrels and other rodents, some bats like the one shown hibernating here, and certain kinds of snakes are known to hibernate. Some animals sleep through hot summer weather or droughts. This is called *aestivation*.

ORGANISMS AND ADAPTED ENVIRONMENT

Animals and plants are adapted to live in their environments in many special ways. For example, polar bears have white fur as camouflage which helps them blend in with their icy and snowy background. This makes it easier to sneak up on the seals on which they prey. They also have thick fur and a thick layer of blubber to help keep them warm in their frigid environment.

INSTINCTIVE BEHAVIORS

Instinctive behaviors are actions that are automatic in an animal and do not have to be taught or learned. Newly hatched sea turtles automatically crawl across the beach towards the ocean with no mother around to show them what to do. Tree squirrels automatically store acorns and nuts during the summer in order to have food in the coming winter. Also, salmon automatically return from the ocean to the freshwater river where they hatched in order to spawn.

CAMOUFLAGE AND MIMICRY

Generally speaking, *camouflage* is when an organism blends in with its surroundings in a way that it cannot be seen as in the case of the flounder blending in with the gravel on the bottom of a lake (Fig. B). *Mimicry* is when an organism resembles something else, like the leaf insect in Fig. A. In these two examples each animal is able to avoid being seen and eaten by a predator. However, sometimes it is the predator that is camouflaged or a mimic which enables it to pounce on its unsuspecting prey.

WARNING COLORATION

Dangerously venomous or poisonous animals often are brightly colored to warn predators that they are best left alone. This is called aposematic coloration. The deadly venomous coral snake (Fig. A.)

has bright red, yellow and black bands that circle its body. The harmless milk snake (Fig. B) mimics the dangerous coral snake which fools predators to leave them alone, too.

COMPETITION BETWEEN DIFFERENT ORGANISMS

Animals and plants have to compete with other species for food or nutrients, water, a place to live, nesting or breeding sites, sunlight in the case of plants, and other factors in the environment that may be scarce or limiting. Also, animals and plants of the same species have to compete with each other for the same things, as well in some cases for the right to breed and reproduce.

GENETICS AND HEREDITY

Genetics is the study of biological inheritance in organisms. Animals generally reproduce with a mother and a father, which both contribute their **genetic** information to offspring. The passing along of genetic traits is also known as **heredity**. The offspring of a mother with red hair and blue eyes with a father who has brown hair and brown eyes may receive any combination of those traits. Another example may be a red fox mating with a brown fox; the offspring may have either brown fur or red fur, and a pack of siblings may have a mixture of inherited traits. This type of inheritance can also be seen in plant life, as pink and white flowered plants may breed together to produce either pink or white flowered offspring, or even special hybrids with blended colors.

INNATE BEHAVIORS

Similar to genetics, there are some behaviors that are innate, or instinctual. Many animals do not nurture their young, but instead, the newborn creatures are capable of fending for themselves. Below are some examples of innate behaviors that are not learned or taught.

- Birds migrate from North to South for the winter to protect themselves from the cold.
- Salmon swim upstream to nesting grounds.
- Some insects migrate and form cocoons to metamorphose.
- Rattlesnakes shake their rattles to warn other animals.

LEARNED BEHAVIORS

Some behaviors and traits may be inherited, but many behaviors must be taught by the parents or pack to the young. Below are some examples of learned or taught behaviors.

- A wolf pack teaches the young wolves how to hunt effectively as a group.
- Some primates use sticks as tools to gather food.
- Dogs learn tricks and commands from their owners.
- Pelicans learn to hunt for fish in groups.
- Humans teach their children words and how to read.

CHANGES THROUGHOUT THE LIFE CYCLE

Many types of plants and animals go through a process of changes throughout their lifespan. This process involves a complete change in how the plant or animal looks and acts during that life stage. In insects and in amphibians, this is called **metamorphosis**.

TOMATO PLANT LIFE CYCLE

Tomato plants undergo a series of life stages, starting at the seed. The **seed** contains all of its own nutrition for the beginning stages of life. Once it is planted, it grows into a **seedling** and starts using photosynthesis to harness the energy for life and growth. When the plant is **mature**, it produces **flowers** which then produce the tomato fruit. The **fruit** contains seeds which then go on to become the next generation for this plant. The tomato plant usually dies after one year, so the next generation comes directly from the seeds of the previous generation.

LIMA BEAN LIFE CYCLE

Lima beans have similar life cycles are similar to that of a tomato plan. It begins are a seed, which grows roots underground. As it grows and emerges from the soil, it becomes a seedling, which eventually becomes an adult lima bean plant. Rather than flowering, it produces leaves and pods, which contain several new seeds. These seeds are known as beans, which can be replanted or cooked for food.

RADISH LIFE CYCLE

Radishes also begin as a seed, which germinates into a sprout. The radish grows large leaves above ground while the root underground also grows large and round. When the plant grows into an adult, it flowers, producing more seeds. The large root underground is generally what most people think of as a radish, and the leaves that grow above ground are known as radish greens. Both the root and the leaves are cooked and eaten.

FROG LIFE CYCLE

Frogs have a very distinctive life cycle. Frogs start out as eggs, which hatch into tadpoles. Tadpoles live and breathe completely in the water using gills and have no legs or arms to walk with. As the tadpole begins to mature, it grows legs and eventually becomes a young frog. The young frogs then emerge from the water and usually live on land and breathe air using lungs. Some frogs are still able to live and breathe underwater throughout their adult life. Frogs then reproduce by laying eggs in the water.

LADY BEETLE AND BUTTERFLY LIFE CYCLES

Lady Beetles, commonly called ladybugs and butterflies start their lives as eggs, which then hatch into a larva, which is most similar to a worm. In butterflies, this is called a caterpillar. The larva usually spends its life eating to build up energy for the change to its next stage. The larva eventually turns into a pupa or a chrysalis, which is a far less active stage. In this change, the larva spins a web around itself, becoming a cocoon. In this stage, the body changes form and eventually, an adult butterfly or ladybug emerges. The adult forms of both of these creatures have wings and are then able to fly and eventually produce new eggs.

CRICKET LIFE CYCLE

Crickets undergo a similar but far less dramatic lifecycle change than metamorphosing insects. They start as eggs, which hatch into **nymph** crickets, which are essentially the same as the adult form of the insect, only smaller and not capable of reproducing yet. As the nymph grows, it eventually comes into adulthood and can then mate and lay eggs.

Practice Test #1

Practice Questions

1. What is the object below used to measure?

   a. Length
   b. Mass
   c. Volume
   d. Temperature

2. Which simple machine was used to raise this flag?

   a. Screw
   b. Pulley
   c. Lever
   d. Inclined plane

3. Which of the following are examples of a predator and prey?

   a. Eagle and rabbit
   b. Rabbit and grass
   c. Grass and tree
   d. Eagle and grass

4. During recess four students ran laps in the gym. The times of their fastest laps are recorded below. Which of the following is a reasonable statement based on the information contained in the chart?

Student	Fastest Lap Time Seconds
Lena	17
Carl	15
Courtney	22
Matthew	25

    a. Courtney likes to run.
    b. Carl ran the fastest.
    c. Lena is taller than Carl.
    d. Matthew is sick.

5. Why do we see the moon cycle through its phases?
    a. The moon is blocked by the sun.
    b. The moon is covered by clouds.
    c. The moon is blocked by the trees.
    d. The moon revolves about the earth.

6. The ice cube below is slowly changing to a liquid. What is the name of this process?

    a. Evaporation
    b. Condensation
    c. Melting
    d. Freezing

7. Where does the energy that drives the water cycle come from?
    a. The sun
    b. The moon
    c. The ocean
    d. The clouds

8. Which of the following activities best shows the importance of tracking weather?
    a. A farmer planting crops
    b. A janitor sweeping the floor
    c. A secretary answering the phone
    d. A doctor performing surgery

9. Which of the following is best described by heavy rains, hail, and lightning?

    a. Landslide
    b. Earthquake
    c. Thunderstorm
    d. Blizzard

10. Which of the materials listed below is a gas?

    a. Milk
    b. Rain
    c. Water
    d. Air

11. How long does it take the earth to make one complete rotation on its axis?

    a. One day
    b. One year
    c. One month
    d. One week

12. About how tall is this tree?

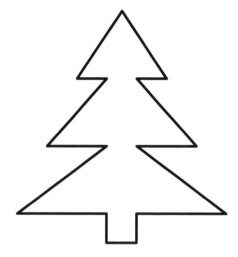

    a. One inch
    b. Two inches
    c. Three inches
    d. Four inches

13. A student sorts her lunch trash into the correct recycling containers. Into which container should she place some aluminum foil?

    a. Glass
    b. Metal
    c. Paper
    d. Plastic

14. **Which of the following would have the most dramatic effect on a woodland habitat?**
    a. Leaves falling to the ground
    b. Moss growing on trees
    c. Squirrels eating nuts
    d. Campers leaving trash

15. **Which of the following is an important plant product?**
    a. Salt
    b. Wood
    c. Iron
    d. Plastic

16. **Which of the following would be the correct units to use for reporting temperature?**

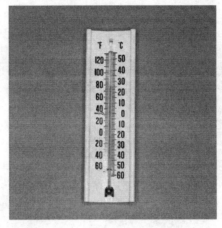

    a. Pounds
    b. Degrees
    c. Feet
    d. Gallons

17. **What is the correct order of the seasons starting with the coldest season?**
    a. Winter, summer, spring, autumn
    b. Winter, autumn, summer, spring
    c. Winter, spring, summer, autumn
    d. Winter, spring, autumn, summer

18. **Which of the following is a renewable source of energy?**
    a. Wind
    b. Natural gas
    c. Crude oil
    d. Coal

19. **Why does an electric can opener hold the top of the can after it is removed?**

    a. The opener is dirty.
    b. The opener is plastic.
    c. The opener is electric.
    d. The opener has a magnet.

20. **Which of the following is true concerning the animals in the table below?**

Chicken	Toad	Goldfish
Lay eggs	Lay eggs	Lay eggs
Lungs	Lungs	Gills
Feathers	Dry skin	Scales

    a. All three animals have feathers.
    b. All three animals lay eggs.
    c. All three animals have lungs.
    d. All three animals have gills.

21. Which of the following is a correct observation concerning the dolls below?

A.   B.

a. Doll A has longer hair than doll B.
b. Doll A is newer than doll B.
c. Doll A is prettier than doll B.
d. Doll A is heavier than doll B.

22. If the trees in a large wooded area are cut and removed to build a new housing subdivision, what will most likely happen to the animals in the area?

a. More food sources will be available.
b. Animals will lose their homes.
c. More water will be available.
d. New animals will move into the area.

23. A student completed an insect collection for his science class. Which of the following insects does he have the fewest of?

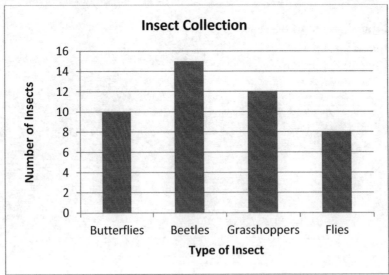

a. Butterflies
b. Beetles
c. Grasshoppers
d. Flies

54

24. Flooding is usually caused by which of the following?

    a. Heavy rains
    b. Lightning
    c. Tornadoes
    d. Rainbows

25. Why does a compass needle point north?

    a. The needle is plastic.
    b. The needle is stuck.
    c. The needle is magnetic.
    d. The needle is shiny.

26. What does the weather instrument shown below measure?

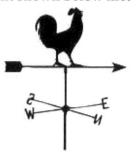

    a. Atmospheric pressure
    b. Temperature
    c. Wind direction
    d. The amount of rainfall

27. Which type of simple machine is this ax?

    a. Pulley
    b. Lever
    c. Inclined plane
    d. Wedge

28. Members of a third grade class selected crickets and then measured the length of their jumps. Data for four students is recorded in the table below.

Student	Distance Cricket Jumped in Centimeters
Rachel	17
Alex	12
Aaron	9
Laura	13

Which student's cricket jumped the shortest distance?

a. Rachel
b. Alex
c. Aaron
d. Laura

29. This butterfly has markings on its wings that look like huge eyes. How does this physical adaptation help the butterfly?

a. The eyespots help the butterfly fly.
b. The eyespots help the butterfly find food.
c. The eyespots help the butterfly scare off predators.
d. The eyespots help the butterfly smell.

30. A student drops a piece of chalk, and it breaks into several pieces. Which of the following properties of the chalk changes?

a. Amount
b. Hardness
c. Color
d. Shape

31. Which of the following would help prevent air pollution?

    a. Carpooling to school
    b. Burning leaves
    c. Using cloth shopping bags
    d. Turning off lights

32. About how many blocks tall is the slide?

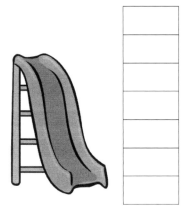

    a. One
    b. Three
    c. Five
    d. Seven

33. Which of the following is a carnivore?

    a. Butterfly
    b. Toadstool
    c. Squirrel
    d. Lion

34. Which of the follow is an effect of the moon on the earth?

    a. Tides
    b. Landslides
    c. Tornadoes
    d. Seasons

35. When a raindrop freezes, what does it change into?

    a. Solid
    b. Water
    c. Liquid
    d. Gas

36. Which of the following processes is NOT part of the water cycle?

    a. Precipitation
    b. Decomposition
    c. Evaporation
    d. Condensation

37. Which of the following would help conserve water?

   a. Turning the water off while brushing our teeth
   b. Recycling plastic bottles
   c. Using cloth shopping bags
   d. Planting a garden

38. A third grade class planted tomato seeds and measured the plant growth after a few weeks. According to this bar graph, which student had the tallest plant?

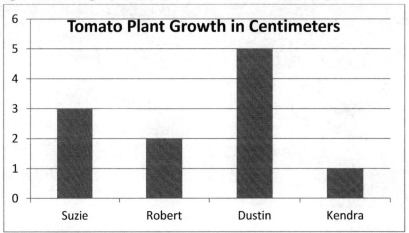

   a. Suzie
   b. Robert
   c. Dustin
   d. Kendra

39. Why do we experience day and night on earth?

   a. Because the moon rotates on its axis
   b. Because clouds cover the sun
   c. Because the earth rotates on its axis
   d. Because the earth revolves around the sun

40. Which of the following is a producer?

   a. Tiger
   b. Goldfish
   c. Worm
   d. Tulip

Answers and Explanations

1. B: Mass. The triple beam balance measures *mass*. A ruler measures length. A graduated cylinder measures volume. A thermometer measures temperature. Therefore, the correct choice is B.

2. B: Pulley. A pulley is a simple machine that has a wheel with a rope wrapped around it. The flag is attached to the rope, which is pulled to raise the flag. Therefore, the correct choice is B.

3. A: Eagle and rabbit. A predator and prey are both animals. The predator eats the prey. An eagle eats a rabbit. The other choices all have at least one plant and are, therefore, incorrect. The correct choice is A.

4. B: Carl ran the fastest. The only information contained in the chart is the time of each student's fastest lap. No information is given as to whether a student likes to run, is tall, or is sick. Therefore, the correct choice is B.

5. D: The moon revolves about the earth. We see the moon's phases because it revolves around the earth. The moon is never blocked by the sun. Clouds and trees may temporarily block our view of the moon, but they do not cause the moon's phases. Therefore, the correct choice is D.

6. C: Melting. Melting occurs when a solid changes to a liquid. Evaporation occurs when a liquid changes into a gas. Condensation occurs when a gas changes into a liquid. Freezing occurs when a liquid changes into a solid. Therefore, the correct choice is C.

7. A: The sun. The sun provides the energy that drives the water cycle. The moon's gravity causes tides. The ocean provides water for the water cycle but not the energy. The clouds are condensed water droplets. Therefore, the correct choice is A.

8. A: A farmer planting crops. A farmer plants crops outside, which depends on the weather. Sweeping the floor, answering the phone, and performing surgery all occur inside. Therefore, the correct choice is A.

9. C: Thunderstorm. Thunderstorms have heavy rain, hail, and lightning. Landslides, earthquakes, and blizzards are not described this way. Therefore, the correct choice is C.

10. D: Air. Milk, rain, and water are liquids. Air is a gas. Therefore, the correct choice is D.

11. A: One day. The earth rotates once every day. The earth revolves around the sun once every year. The moon cycles through its phases once every month. A week is seven days. Therefore, the correct choice is A.

12. B: Two inches. The tree is about two inches tall. Therefore, the correct answer is B.

13. B: Metal. Aluminum is a metal. Aluminum is not glass, paper, or plastic. Therefore, the correct choice is B.

14. D: Campers leaving trash. Leaves falling, moss growing, and squirrels eating are all natural events in a woodland habitat. Campers leaving trash is littering and can be harmful to the environment. Therefore, the correct choice is D.

15. B: Wood. Wood is a plant product. Salt is a substance found in sea water. Iron is a metal. Plastic is man-made. Therefore, the correct choice is B.

16. B: Degrees. Temperature is measured in degrees. Weight is measured in pounds. Length is measured in feet. Volume is measured in gallons. Therefore, the correct choice is B.

17. C: Winter, spring, summer, autumn. The correct order of the seasons is winter, spring, summer, and autumn, as in answer choice C. All the other answer choices mix up the order of seasons.

18. A: Wind. Wind is a renewable source of energy, because there will always be wind. Natural gas, crude oil, and coal will eventually run out and are nonrenewable. Therefore, the correct choice is A.

19. D: The opener has a magnet. Can lids remain on the can opener because the lid is metal and the opener has a magnet, which pulls the metal lid toward it. Therefore, the correct choice is D.

20. B: All three animals lay eggs. The only true statement is that all three animals lay eggs. They do not all have feathers, lungs, or gills. Therefore, the correct choice is B.

21. A: Doll A has longer hair than doll B. The only factually correct observation offered is that doll A has longer hair than doll B. Which doll is newer or heavier cannot be determined from this picture, and prettiness is not a measurable quantity. Therefore, the correct answer is A.

22. B: Animals will lose their homes. If the wooded area is cleared, habitats will be destroyed, and animals will lose their homes. Clearing the area is unlikely to cause an increase in available water or food, or the arrival of new wildlife. Therefore, the correct answer is B.

23. D: Flies. The student included 10 butterflies, 15 beetles, 12 grasshoppers, and only 8 flies. Therefore, the correct choice is D.

24. A: Heavy rains. Heavy rains may cause flooding. Lightning, tornadoes, and rainbows are associated with thunderstorms but do not cause flooding. Therefore, the correct choice is A.

25. C: The needle is magnetic. A compass needle points north because it is magnetic, as is the magnetic north pole. Therefore, the correct choice is C.

26. C: Wind direction. The instrument is a wind vane. Wind vanes measure wind direction. Barometers measure atmospheric pressure. Thermometers measure temperature. Rain gauges measure the amount of rainfall. Therefore, the correct choice is C.

27. D: Wedge. A pulley is a kind of wheel with raised edges that is used with a rope or cable to make it easier to lift heavy objects. A lever is a bar or pole used on top of a support called a fulcrum to lift or pry. An inclined plane is a slanted surface that connects a lower level to a higher one. A wedge splits materials apart, as the ax blade does the wood. Therefore, the correct answer is D.

28. C: Aaron. Rachel's cricket jumped 17 centimeters. Alex's cricket jumped 12 centimeters. Aaron's cricket jumped 9 centimeters. Laura's cricket jumped 13 centimeters. Nine centimeters is the shortest distance listed. Therefore, the correct choice is C.

29. C: The eyespots help the butterfly scare off predators. Butterflies with the two large eyespots will suddenly show them to predators to scare them off. The eyespots do not help them fly, find food, or smell. Therefore, the correct choice is C.

30. D: Shape. When the chalk breaks, its amount, hardness, and color remain the same. The shape, however, changes. Therefore, the correct choice is D.

31. A: Carpooling to school. Carpooling would reduce the number of cars being driven and would reduce air pollution. Burning leaves would increase air pollution. While using cloth shopping bags and turning off lights are both beneficial, neither helps reduce air pollution. Therefore, the correct choice is A.

32. C: Five. The slide is about five blocks tall. Therefore, the correct choice is C.

33. D: Lion. Carnivores are animals that eat meat. Butterflies and squirrels are plant eaters, or herbivores. Toadstools are decomposers. Lions eat other animals. Therefore, the correct choice is D.

34. A: Tides. The moon's gravity causes tides. The moon does not cause landslides, tornadoes, or seasons. Therefore, the correct choice is A.

35. A: Solid. When a raindrop freezes, it changes from a liquid into a solid. Therefore, the correct answer is A.

36. B: Decomposition. Precipitation, evaporation, and condensation are all parts of the water cycle. Decomposition is not part of the water cycle. Therefore, the correct choice is B.

37. A: Turning the water off while brushing our teeth. Recycling plastic bottles, using cloth shopping bags, and planting a garden are responsible activities, but do not help conserve water. Turning the water off while brushing our teeth would help conserve water. Therefore, the correct answer is A.

38. C: Dustin. Dustin's plant grew five centimeters, while the other plants only grew three centimeters, two centimeters, and one centimeter. Therefore, the correct answer is C.

39. C: Because the earth rotates on its axis. We experience day and night because the earth rotates on its axis. The moon's rotation causes the phases of the moon. The clouds may make it periodically dimmer but do not cause day and night. Because of the earth's tilted axis, seasons occur during the earth's revolution about the sun. Therefore, the correct choice is C.

40. D: Tulip. A tiger, a goldfish, and a worm are all animals and cannot be producers. A tulip is a plant, so it is a producer. Therefore, the correct answer is D.

Practice Test #2

Practice Questions

1. Why are some paperclips on the top of the container?

    a. The lid is a magnet.
    b. The paperclips are too big to fit through the hole.
    c. The top is sticky.
    d. The paperclips are plastic.

2. What is the object below used to measure?

    a. Temperature
    b. Volume
    c. Mass
    d. Length

3. Which of the following is a decomposer?

    a. Octopus
    b. Seal
    c. Mold
    d. Cactus

4. What causes Earth to follow a pattern of day and night?

    a. The moon blocks the sun.
    b. The earth rotates once every 24 hours.
    c. The sun is covered by clouds.
    d. The earth revolves around the sun.

5. Which of the following objects is made from a material that is attracted to a magnet?

a.

b.

c.

d.

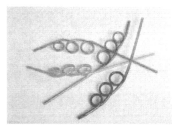

6. Which of the following is a factual observation for the dogs pictured below?

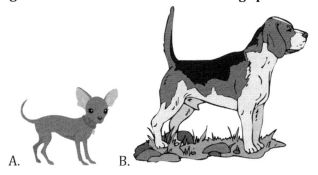

A.   B.

    a.   Dog A is nicer than dog B.
    b.   Dog A is smarter than dog B.
    c.   Dog A is cuter than dog B.
    d.   Dog A is smaller than dog B.

7. During the water cycle, what is it called when liquid water is heated and is changed to a gas?

    a.   Erosion
    b.   Condensation
    c.   Precipitation
    d.   Evaporation

8. Some students held a free throw shooting contest during recess. The number of free throws that were made out of 10 attempts is recorded in the chart below. Which of the following is a reasonable statement to make based on the information in the chart?

Student	Number of Free Throws Made Out of 10 Tries
Lydia	8
Conner	2
Hannah	7
Robert	10

    a. Lydia is short.
    b. Hannah loves basketball.
    c. Robert made every free throw.
    d. Conner needs glasses.

9. Which of the following would have a negative effect on our environment?

    a. Burning leaves
    b. Riding bikes
    c. Planting a garden
    d. Playing baseball

10. A student helps her family sort trash into the correct recycling bins. Into which bin should she place the empty soup cans?

    a. Plastic
    b. Paper
    c. Glass
    d. Metal

11. Which of the following units should be used to report weight?

    a. Inches
    b. Pounds
    c. Degrees
    d. Gallons

12. The tree shown below loses its leaves every year and is now budding again. Which season is this?

   a. Summer
   b. Autumn
   c. Winter
   d. Spring

13. Which of the materials listed below is a liquid?

   a. Water
   b. Snow
   c. Ice
   d. Steam

14. Which of the following is a nonrenewable source of energy?

   a. Sunlight
   b. Coal
   c. Wind
   d. Trees

15. How long does it take the earth to revolve once around the sun?

   a. One day
   b. One week
   c. One month
   d. One year

16. Droughts are caused by which of the following?

   a. Very little rain
   b. Volcanic eruptions
   c. High winds
   d. Lightning strikes

17. Which type of simple machine is this seesaw?

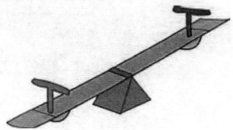

    a. Inclined plane
    b. Lever
    c. Wedge
    d. Wheel and axle

18. Which two animals share a predator and prey relationship?
    a. Bird and flower seed
    b. Fish and algae
    c. Mushroom and rotten log
    d. Lion and zebra

19. The United States regularly cycles through four seasons. About how many months does each season last?
    a. One
    b. Two
    c. Three
    d. Four

20. Characteristics of three different animals are shown in the table below.

Rabbit	Lion	Eagle
Herbivore	Carnivore	Carnivore
Lungs	Lungs	Lungs
Fur	Fur	Feathers

Which of the following is true based on the information given in the table?
    a. All three animals have fur.
    b. All three animals have lungs.
    c. All three animals are carnivores.
    d. All three animals are herbivores.

21. Which of the following correctly lists <u>only</u> components of soil?
    a. Rock, cotton, silk, sand, humus
    b. Rock, clay, iron, gold, silt
    c. Rock, clay, silt, sand, humus
    d. Rock, plastic, wood, silt, humus

22. A third grade class planted corn seeds and measured the height of the plants after several weeks. The data for four of the students was recorded in the table below. Which student's plant was the shortest?

Student	Corn Plant Height (Inches)
Steven	3
Natalie	5
Brianna	7
Josh	4

   a. Steven
   b. Natalie
   c. Brianna
   d. Josh

23. What does one day represent?
   a. The amount of time for the moon to revolve around the earth
   b. The amount of time for the earth to rotate once on its axis
   c. The amount of time for the earth to revolve around the sun
   d. The amount of time for the sun to rotate once on its axis

24. The earth's water cycle requires large amounts of energy. Where does this energy come from?
   a. The sun
   b. The moon
   c. The clouds
   d. The ocean

25. About how many blocks tall is this tower?

    a. Two
    b. Three
    c. Four
    d. Five

26. Why does the state of Virginia experience the seasons spring, summer, autumn, and winter?

    a. The moon causes tides.
    b. The clouds block the sun.
    c. The earth is always tilted on its axis.
    d. Rain falls from clouds.

27. Sally planted a garden. The graph below shows how many rows of each type of plant she planted.

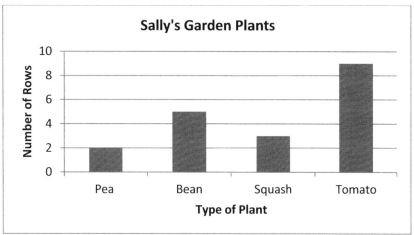

Which of the following is the plant with the least amount of rows planted?

a. Pea
b. Bean
c. Squash
d. Tomato

28. Which of the following represents the end of a frog's life cycle?

a. The tadpole becomes an adult frog.
b. The egg becomes a tadpole.
c. The frog hatches from its egg.
d. The frog dies.

29. What occurs when a liquid changes into a gas?

a. Melting
b. Freezing
c. Evaporation
d. Condensation

30. What does this weather instrument measure?

a. Wind direction
b. Temperature
c. Amount of rainfall
d. Length

69

31. A baseball crashes into a stained-glass window and shatters the glass. Which of the following properties of the glass changes?

    a. Shape of the glass
    b. Amount of glass
    c. Materials in the glass
    d. Color of the glass

32. A bean plant begins its life cycle as which of the following?

    a. Leaf
    b. Root
    c. Stem
    d. Seed

33. About how long is this car from bumper to bumper?

    a. One inch
    b. Two inches
    c. Three inches
    d. Four inches

34. Which of the following helps conserve trees?

    a. Turning the lights out when we leave a room
    b. Watering our lawns only in the morning
    c. Walking instead of riding in cars
    d. Recycling newspapers and magazines

35. Which of the following dissolves in water?

    a. Wood
    b. Plastic
    c. Salt
    d. Sand

36. A third grade science class made paper airplanes and then measured the distance the airplanes flew. According to this bar graph, which student made the airplane that flew the farthest?

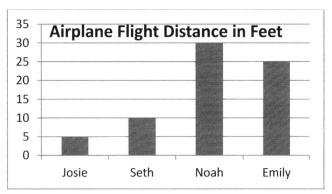

a. Josie
b. Seth
c. Noah
d. Emily

37. Evaporation, precipitation, and condensation are all important parts of which cycle?
   a. Erosion cycle
   b. Animal cycle
   c. Water cycle
   d. Plant cycle

38. What word best describes a deer?
   a. Producer
   b. Decomposer
   c. Carnivore
   d. Herbivore

39. Which unit would be the most appropriate to indicate the volume of water in a bathtub?

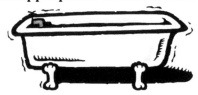

   a. Feet
   b. Gallons
   c. Degrees
   d. Pounds

40. When a popsicle melts, what does it change into?
   a. Liquid
   b. Ice
   c. Gas
   d. Solid

Answers and Explanations

1. A: The lid is a magnet. The lid contains a magnet that attracts the metal paperclips. The top is not sticky, nor are the paperclips too big to fit through the gap. Therefore, the correct choice is A.

2. B: Volume. A graduated cylinder measures volume. A thermometer measures temperature. A balance measures mass. A ruler measures length. Therefore, the correct choice is B.

3. C: Mold. An octopus and a seal are carnivores. A cactus is a producer. Mold is a decomposer. Therefore, the correct choice is C.

4. B: The earth rotates once every 24 hours. The earth's rotation causes the pattern of day and night. When the moon blocks the sun, an eclipse occurs. Clouds only temporarily block sun. The earth's yearly revolution around the sun contributes to our having seasons. Therefore, the correct choice is B.

5. A: Paperclip. Paperclips are made of metal. The other materials shown are paper, wood, and plastic, which are not attracted to magnets. Therefore, the correct choice is A.

6. D: Dog A is smaller than dog B. The only fact-based observation that can be made from the pictures shown is that dog A is smaller than dog B. Which dog is nicer, cuter, or smarter is either a matter of opinion or cannot be determined simply by looking. Therefore, the correct choice is D.

7. D: Evaporation. Evaporation occurs when a liquid changes to a gas. Condensation occurs when a gas changes into a liquid. Precipitation is any form of water that falls from the sky. Erosion is the removal of rock and soil. Therefore, the correct choice is D.

8. C: Robert made every free throw. The only information contained in the chart is how many free throws each student made. The chart does not provide information about any student's height, eyesight, or feelings about basketball. Therefore, the correct choice is C.

9. A: Burning leaves. Riding bikes, planting a garden, and playing baseball will not hurt the environment. Burning leaves causes air pollution. Therefore, the correct choice is A.

10. D: Metal. Soup cans are made of metal. Soup cans are not plastic, paper, or glass. Therefore, the correct choice is D.

11. B: Pounds. Weight is measured in pounds. Length is measured in inches. Temperature is measured in degrees. Volume is measured in gallons. Therefore, the correct choice is B.

12. D: Spring. Deciduous trees lose their leaves every autumn and bud again every spring. Therefore, the correct choice is D.

13. A: Water. Water is a liquid. Snow and ice are solids. Steam is a gas. Therefore, the correct answer is A.

14. B: Coal. Sunlight and wind will never run out. Trees can be replanted. Sunlight, wind, and trees are *renewable* sources of energy. The coal supply will eventually be depleted. Therefore, the correct choice is B.

15. D: One year. The earth revolves around the sun once every 365 days, which is one year. A day, week, and month are much shorter. Therefore, the correct choice is D.

16. A: Very little rain. Droughts may occur during long periods of very little rain. Volcanic eruptions, high winds, and lightning strikes do not cause droughts. Therefore, the correct choice is A.

17. B: Lever. A seesaw is a flat board that pivots on a fulcrum, meaning that a seesaw is a lever. Therefore, the correct choice is B.

18. D: Lion and zebra. A predator and prey are both animals. The predator eats the prey. Choice D is the only choice with two animals, and lions do hunt and eat zebras. Therefore, the correct choice is D.

19. C: Three. The four seasons each last about three months. Twelve months makes one full cycle. Therefore, the correct choice is C.

20. B: All three animals have lungs. They do not all have fur. They are not all carnivores. They are not all herbivores. Therefore, the correct choice is B.

21. C: Rock, clay, silt, sand, humus. Rock, clay, silt, sand, and humus are all natural components of soil. Cotton and wood come from plants. Silk comes from animals. Iron and gold are metals. Plastic is manmade. Therefore, the correct choice is C.

22. A: Steven. Steven's plant was three inches tall. Natalie's plant was five inches tall. Brianna's plant was seven inches tall. Josh's plant was four inches tall. Therefore, the correct choice is A.

23. B: The amount of time for the earth to rotate once on its axis. One day is the time it takes the earth to rotate completely one time. One year is the time it takes the earth to revolve around the sun once. One month is the amount of time it takes the moon to orbit the earth and to complete one rotation.

24. A: The sun. The sun provides the energy that drives the earth's water cycle. The energy does not come from the moon, the clouds, or the ocean. Therefore, the correct choice is A.

25. C: Four. The tower is about four blocks high. Therefore, the correct choice is C.

26. C: The earth is always tilted on its axis. The tilt of the earth's axis causes the seasons. The moon, rain, and clouds do not cause seasons. Therefore, the correct choice is C.

27. A: Pea. Sally planted two rows of peas, five rows of beans, three rows of squash, and nine rows of tomatoes. Therefore, the correct choice is A.

28. D: The frog dies. All animal life cycles end with death. Therefore, the correct answer is D.

29. C: Evaporation. Evaporation is when a liquid changes into a gas. Melting is when a solid changes into a liquid. Freezing is when a liquid changes into a solid. Condensation is when a gas changes into a liquid. Therefore, the correct choice is C.

30. B: Temperature. A thermometer measures temperature. A wind vane measures wind direction. A rain gauge measures the amount of rainfall. A ruler measures length. Therefore, the correct choice is B.

31. A: Shape of the glass. When the glass breaks, the shape changes. The amount of the glass, the materials in the glass, and the color of the glass do not change. Therefore, the correct choice is A.

32. D: Seed. Bean plants begin their lives as seeds. Then they grow roots, stems, and leaves. Therefore, the correct choice is D.

33. B: Two inches. The car is about two inches long. Therefore, the correct choice is B.

34. D: Recycling newspapers and magazines. Turning the lights out when we leave a room helps conserve energy. Watering our lawns only in the morning helps conserve water. Walking instead of riding in cars helps prevent pollution. Recycling newspapers and magazines helps conserve trees. Therefore, the correct choice is D.

35. C: Salt. Salt dissolves in water. Wood, plastic, and sand do not dissolve in water. Therefore, the correct choice is C.

36. C: Noah. According to the bar graph, Josie's plane flew five feet. Seth's plane flew 10 feet. Noah's plane flew 30 feet. Emily's plane flew 25 feet. Noah's plane flew the farthest. Therefore, the correct choice is C.

37. C: Water cycle. Evaporation, precipitation, and condensation are all components of the water cycle. Therefore, the correct choice is C.

38. D: Herbivore. Plants are producers. Bacteria and fungi are decomposers. Animals that eat other animals are carnivores. Herbivores eat plants. A deer eats various types of plants and acorns. Therefore, the correct choice is D.

39. B: Gallons. Volume is measured in gallons. Length is measured in feet. Temperature is measured in degrees. Weight is measured in pounds. Therefore, the correct choice is B.

40. A: Liquid. When a popsicle melts, it changes from a solid to a liquid. Therefore, the correct answer is A.

How to Overcome Test Anxiety

Just the thought of taking a test is enough to make most people a little nervous. A test is an important event that can have a long-term impact on your future, so it's important to take it seriously and it's natural to feel anxious about performing well. But just because anxiety is normal, that doesn't mean that it's helpful in test taking, or that you should simply accept it as part of your life. Anxiety can have a variety of effects. These effects can be mild, like making you feel slightly nervous, or severe, like blocking your ability to focus or remember even a simple detail.

If you experience test anxiety—whether severe or mild—it's important to know how to beat it. To discover this, first you need to understand what causes test anxiety.

Causes of Test Anxiety

While we often think of anxiety as an uncontrollable emotional state, it can actually be caused by simple, practical things. One of the most common causes of test anxiety is that a person does not feel adequately prepared for their test. This feeling can be the result of many different issues such as poor study habits or lack of organization, but the most common culprit is time management. Starting to study too late, failing to organize your study time to cover all of the material, or being distracted while you study will mean that you're not well prepared for the test. This may lead to cramming the night before, which will cause you to be physically and mentally exhausted for the test. Poor time management also contributes to feelings of stress, fear, and hopelessness as you realize you are not well prepared but don't know what to do about it.

Other times, test anxiety is not related to your preparation for the test but comes from unresolved fear. This may be a past failure on a test, or poor performance on tests in general. It may come from comparing yourself to others who seem to be performing better or from the stress of living up to expectations. Anxiety may be driven by fears of the future—how failure on this test would affect your educational and career goals. These fears are often completely irrational, but they can still negatively impact your test performance.

> **Review Video: 3 Reasons You Have Test Anxiety**
> Visit mometrix.com/academy and enter code: 428468

Elements of Test Anxiety

As mentioned earlier, test anxiety is considered to be an emotional state, but it has physical and mental components as well. Sometimes you may not even realize that you are suffering from test anxiety until you notice the physical symptoms. These can include trembling hands, rapid heartbeat, sweating, nausea, and tense muscles. Extreme anxiety may lead to fainting or vomiting. Obviously, any of these symptoms can have a negative impact on testing. It is important to recognize them as soon as they begin to occur so that you can address the problem before it damages your performance.

> **Review Video: 3 Ways to Tell You Have Test Anxiety**
> Visit mometrix.com/academy and enter code: 927847

The mental components of test anxiety include trouble focusing and inability to remember learned information. During a test, your mind is on high alert, which can help you recall information and stay focused for an extended period of time. However, anxiety interferes with your mind's natural processes, causing you to blank out, even on the questions you know well. The strain of testing during anxiety makes it difficult to stay focused, especially on a test that may take several hours. Extreme anxiety can take a huge mental toll, making it difficult not only to recall test information but even to understand the test questions or pull your thoughts together.

> **Review Video: How Test Anxiety Affects Memory**
> Visit mometrix.com/academy and enter code: 609003

Effects of Test Anxiety

Test anxiety is like a disease—if left untreated, it will get progressively worse. Anxiety leads to poor performance, and this reinforces the feelings of fear and failure, which in turn lead to poor performances on subsequent tests. It can grow from a mild nervousness to a crippling condition. If allowed to progress, test anxiety can have a big impact on your schooling, and consequently on your future.

Test anxiety can spread to other parts of your life. Anxiety on tests can become anxiety in any stressful situation, and blanking on a test can turn into panicking in a job situation. But fortunately, you don't have to let anxiety rule your testing and determine your grades. There are a number of relatively simple steps you can take to move past anxiety and function normally on a test and in the rest of life.

> **Review Video: How Test Anxiety Impacts Your Grades**
> Visit mometrix.com/academy and enter code: 939819

Physical Steps for Beating Test Anxiety

While test anxiety is a serious problem, the good news is that it can be overcome. It doesn't have to control your ability to think and remember information. While it may take time, you can begin taking steps today to beat anxiety.

Just as your first hint that you may be struggling with anxiety comes from the physical symptoms, the first step to treating it is also physical. Rest is crucial for having a clear, strong mind. If you are tired, it is much easier to give in to anxiety. But if you establish good sleep habits, your body and mind will be ready to perform optimally, without the strain of exhaustion. Additionally, sleeping well helps you to retain information better, so you're more likely to recall the answers when you see the test questions.

Getting good sleep means more than going to bed on time. It's important to allow your brain time to relax. Take study breaks from time to time so it doesn't get overworked, and don't study right before bed. Take time to rest your mind before trying to rest your body, or you may find it difficult to fall asleep.

> **Review Video: The Importance of Sleep for Your Brain**
> Visit mometrix.com/academy and enter code: 319338

Along with sleep, other aspects of physical health are important in preparing for a test. Good nutrition is vital for good brain function. Sugary foods and drinks may give a burst of energy but this burst is followed by a crash, both physically and emotionally. Instead, fuel your body with protein and vitamin-rich foods.

Also, drink plenty of water. Dehydration can lead to headaches and exhaustion, especially if your brain is already under stress from the rigors of the test. Particularly if your test is a long one, drink water during the breaks. And if possible, take an energy-boosting snack to eat between sections.

> **Review Video: How Diet Can Affect your Mood**
> Visit mometrix.com/academy and enter code: 624317

Along with sleep and diet, a third important part of physical health is exercise. Maintaining a steady workout schedule is helpful, but even taking 5-minute study breaks to walk can help get your blood pumping faster and clear your head. Exercise also releases endorphins, which contribute to a positive feeling and can help combat test anxiety.

When you nurture your physical health, you are also contributing to your mental health. If your body is healthy, your mind is much more likely to be healthy as well. So take time to rest, nourish your body with healthy food and water, and get moving as much as possible. Taking these physical steps will make you stronger and more able to take the mental steps necessary to overcome test anxiety.

Mental Steps for Beating Test Anxiety

Working on the mental side of test anxiety can be more challenging, but as with the physical side, there are clear steps you can take to overcome it. As mentioned earlier, test anxiety often stems from lack of preparation, so the obvious solution is to prepare for the test. Effective studying may be the most important weapon you have for beating test anxiety, but you can and should employ several other mental tools to combat fear.

First, boost your confidence by reminding yourself of past success—tests or projects that you aced. If you're putting as much effort into preparing for this test as you did for those, there's no reason you should expect to fail here. Work hard to prepare; then trust your preparation.

Second, surround yourself with encouraging people. It can be helpful to find a study group, but be sure that the people you're around will encourage a positive attitude. If you spend time with others who are anxious or cynical, this will only contribute to your own anxiety. Look for others who are motivated to study hard from a desire to succeed, not from a fear of failure.

Third, reward yourself. A test is physically and mentally tiring, even without anxiety, and it can be helpful to have something to look forward to. Plan an activity following the test, regardless of the outcome, such as going to a movie or getting ice cream.

When you are taking the test, if you find yourself beginning to feel anxious, remind yourself that you know the material. Visualize successfully completing the test. Then take a few deep, relaxing breaths and return to it. Work through the questions carefully but with confidence, knowing that you are capable of succeeding.

Developing a healthy mental approach to test taking will also aid in other areas of life. Test anxiety affects more than just the actual test—it can be damaging to your mental health and even contribute to depression. It's important to beat test anxiety before it becomes a problem for more than testing.

> **Review Video: <u>Test Anxiety and Depression</u>**
> Visit mometrix.com/academy and enter code: 904704

Study Strategy

Being prepared for the test is necessary to combat anxiety, but what does being prepared look like? You may study for hours on end and still not feel prepared. What you need is a strategy for test prep. The next few pages outline our recommended steps to help you plan out and conquer the challenge of preparation.

STEP 1: SCOPE OUT THE TEST

Learn everything you can about the format (multiple choice, essay, etc.) and what will be on the test. Gather any study materials, course outlines, or sample exams that may be available. Not only will this help you to prepare, but knowing what to expect can help to alleviate test anxiety.

STEP 2: MAP OUT THE MATERIAL

Look through the textbook or study guide and make note of how many chapters or sections it has. Then divide these over the time you have. For example, if a book has 15 chapters and you have five days to study, you need to cover three chapters each day. Even better, if you have the time, leave an extra day at the end for overall review after you have gone through the material in depth.

If time is limited, you may need to prioritize the material. Look through it and make note of which sections you think you already have a good grasp on, and which need review. While you are studying, skim quickly through the familiar sections and take more time on the challenging parts. Write out your plan so you don't get lost as you go. Having a written plan also helps you feel more in control of the study, so anxiety is less likely to arise from feeling overwhelmed at the amount to cover.

STEP 3: GATHER YOUR TOOLS

Decide what study method works best for you. Do you prefer to highlight in the book as you study and then go back over the highlighted portions? Or do you type out notes of the important information? Or is it helpful to make flashcards that you can carry with you? Assemble the pens, index cards, highlighters, post-it notes, and any other materials you may need so you won't be distracted by getting up to find things while you study.

If you're having a hard time retaining the information or organizing your notes, experiment with different methods. For example, try color-coding by subject with colored pens, highlighters, or post-it notes. If you learn better by hearing, try recording yourself reading your notes so you can listen while in the car, working out, or simply sitting at your desk. Ask a friend to quiz you from your flashcards, or try teaching someone the material to solidify it in your mind.

STEP 4: CREATE YOUR ENVIRONMENT

It's important to avoid distractions while you study. This includes both the obvious distractions like visitors and the subtle distractions like an uncomfortable chair (or a too-comfortable couch that makes you want to fall asleep). Set up the best study environment possible: good lighting and a comfortable work area. If background music helps you focus, you may want to turn it on, but otherwise keep the room quiet. If you are using a computer to take notes, be sure you don't have any other windows open, especially applications like social media, games, or anything else that could distract you. Silence your phone and turn off notifications. Be sure to keep water close by so you stay hydrated while you study (but avoid unhealthy drinks and snacks).

Also, take into account the best time of day to study. Are you freshest first thing in the morning? Try to set aside some time then to work through the material. Is your mind clearer in the afternoon or evening? Schedule your study session then. Another method is to study at the same time of day that you will take the test, so that your brain gets used to working on the material at that time and will be ready to focus at test time.

STEP 5: STUDY!

Once you have done all the study preparation, it's time to settle into the actual studying. Sit down, take a few moments to settle your mind so you can focus, and begin to follow your study plan. Don't give in to distractions or let yourself procrastinate. This is your time to prepare so you'll be ready to fearlessly approach the test. Make the most of the time and stay focused.

Of course, you don't want to burn out. If you study too long you may find that you're not retaining the information very well. Take regular study breaks. For example, taking five minutes out of every hour to walk briskly, breathing deeply and swinging your arms, can help your mind stay fresh.

As you get to the end of each chapter or section, it's a good idea to do a quick review. Remind yourself of what you learned and work on any difficult parts. When you feel that you've mastered the material, move on to the next part. At the end of your study session, briefly skim through your notes again.

But while review is helpful, cramming last minute is NOT. If at all possible, work ahead so that you won't need to fit all your study into the last day. Cramming overloads your brain with more information than it can process and retain, and your tired mind may struggle to recall even previously learned information when it is overwhelmed with last-minute study. Also, the urgent nature of cramming and the stress placed on your brain contribute to anxiety. You'll be more likely to go to the test feeling unprepared and having trouble thinking clearly.

So don't cram, and don't stay up late before the test, even just to review your notes at a leisurely pace. Your brain needs rest more than it needs to go over the information again. In fact, plan to finish your studies by noon or early afternoon the day before the test. Give your brain the rest of the day to relax or focus on other things, and get a good night's sleep. Then you will be fresh for the test and better able to recall what you've studied.

STEP 6: TAKE A PRACTICE TEST

Many courses offer sample tests, either online or in the study materials. This is an excellent resource to check whether you have mastered the material, as well as to prepare for the test format and environment.

Check the test format ahead of time: the number of questions, the type (multiple choice, free response, etc.), and the time limit. Then create a plan for working through them. For example, if you have 30 minutes to take a 60-question test, your limit is 30 seconds per question. Spend less time on the questions you know well so that you can take more time on the difficult ones.

If you have time to take several practice tests, take the first one open book, with no time limit. Work through the questions at your own pace and make sure you fully understand them. Gradually work up to taking a test under test conditions: sit at a desk with all study materials put away and set a timer. Pace yourself to make sure you finish the test with time to spare and go back to check your answers if you have time.

After each test, check your answers. On the questions you missed, be sure you understand why you missed them. Did you misread the question (tests can use tricky wording)? Did you forget the information? Or was it something you hadn't learned? Go back and study any shaky areas that the practice tests reveal.

Taking these tests not only helps with your grade, but also aids in combating test anxiety. If you're already used to the test conditions, you're less likely to worry about it, and working through tests until you're scoring well gives you a confidence boost. Go through the practice tests until you feel comfortable, and then you can go into the test knowing that you're ready for it.

Test Tips

On test day, you should be confident, knowing that you've prepared well and are ready to answer the questions. But aside from preparation, there are several test day strategies you can employ to maximize your performance.

First, as stated before, get a good night's sleep the night before the test (and for several nights before that, if possible). Go into the test with a fresh, alert mind rather than staying up late to study.

Try not to change too much about your normal routine on the day of the test. It's important to eat a nutritious breakfast, but if you normally don't eat breakfast at all, consider eating just a protein bar. If you're a coffee drinker, go ahead and have your normal coffee. Just make sure you time it so that the caffeine doesn't wear off right in the middle of your test. Avoid sugary beverages, and drink enough water to stay hydrated but not so much that you need a restroom break 10 minutes into the test. If your test isn't first thing in the morning, consider going for a walk or doing a light workout before the test to get your blood flowing.

Allow yourself enough time to get ready, and leave for the test with plenty of time to spare so you won't have the anxiety of scrambling to arrive in time. Another reason to be early is to select a good seat. It's helpful to sit away from doors and windows, which can be distracting. Find a good seat, get out your supplies, and settle your mind before the test begins.

When the test begins, start by going over the instructions carefully, even if you already know what to expect. Make sure you avoid any careless mistakes by following the directions.

Then begin working through the questions, pacing yourself as you've practiced. If you're not sure on an answer, don't spend too much time on it, and don't let it shake your confidence. Either skip it and come back later, or eliminate as many wrong answers as possible and guess among the remaining ones. Don't dwell on these questions as you continue—put them out of your mind and focus on what lies ahead.

Be sure to read all of the answer choices, even if you're sure the first one is the right answer. Sometimes you'll find a better one if you keep reading. But don't second-guess yourself if you do immediately know the answer. Your gut instinct is usually right. Don't let test anxiety rob you of the information you know.

If you have time at the end of the test (and if the test format allows), go back and review your answers. Be cautious about changing any, since your first instinct tends to be correct, but make sure you didn't misread any of the questions or accidentally mark the wrong answer choice. Look over any you skipped and make an educated guess.

At the end, leave the test feeling confident. You've done your best, so don't waste time worrying about your performance or wishing you could change anything. Instead, celebrate the successful completion of this test. And finally, use this test to learn how to deal with anxiety even better next time.

> **Review Video: 5 Tips to Beat Test Anxiety**
> Visit mometrix.com/academy and enter code: 570656

Important Qualification

Not all anxiety is created equal. If your test anxiety is causing major issues in your life beyond the classroom or testing center, or if you are experiencing troubling physical symptoms related to your anxiety, it may be a sign of a serious physiological or psychological condition. If this sounds like your situation, we strongly encourage you to seek professional help.

How to Overcome Your Fear of Math

The word *math* is enough to strike fear into most hearts. How many of us have memories of sitting through confusing lectures, wrestling over mind-numbing homework, or taking tests that still seem incomprehensible even after hours of study? Years after graduation, many still shudder at these memories.

The fact is, math is not just a classroom subject. It has real-world implications that you face every day, whether you realize it or not. This may be balancing your monthly budget, deciding how many supplies to buy for a project, or simply splitting a meal check with friends. The idea of daily confrontations with math can be so paralyzing that some develop a condition known as *math anxiety*.

But you do NOT need to be paralyzed by this anxiety! In fact, while you may have thought all your life that you're not good at math, or that your brain isn't wired to understand it, the truth is that you may have been conditioned to think this way. From your earliest school days, the way you were taught affected the way you viewed different subjects. And the way math has been taught has changed.

Several decades ago, there was a shift in American math classrooms. The focus changed from traditional problem-solving to a conceptual view of topics, de-emphasizing the importance of learning the basics and building on them. The solid foundation necessary for math progression and confidence was undermined. Math became more of a vague concept than a concrete idea. Today, it is common to think of math, not as a straightforward system, but as a mysterious, complicated method that can't be fully understood unless you're a genius.

This is why you may still have nightmares about being called on to answer a difficult problem in front of the class. Math anxiety is a very real, though unnecessary, fear.

Math anxiety may begin with a single class period. Let's say you missed a day in 6th grade math and never quite understood the concept that was taught while you were gone. Since math is cumulative, with each new concept building on past ones, this could very well affect the rest of your math career. Without that one day's knowledge, it will be difficult to understand any other concepts that link to it. Rather than realizing that you're just missing one key piece, you may begin to believe that you're simply not capable of understanding math.

This belief can change the way you approach other classes, career options, and everyday life experiences, if you become anxious at the thought that math might be required. A student who loves science may choose a different path of study upon realizing that multiple math classes will be required for a degree. An aspiring medical student may hesitate at the thought of going through the necessary math classes. For some this anxiety escalates into a more extreme state known as *math phobia*.

Math anxiety is challenging to address because it is rooted deeply and may come from a variety of causes: an embarrassing moment in class, a teacher who did not explain concepts well and contributed to a shaky foundation, or a failed test that contributed to the belief of math failure.

These causes add up over time, encouraged by society's popular view that math is hard and unpleasant. Eventually a person comes to firmly believe that he or she is simply bad at math. This belief makes it difficult to grasp new concepts or even remember old ones. Homework and test grades begin to slip, which only confirms the belief. The poor performance is not due to lack of ability but is caused by math anxiety.

Math anxiety is an emotional issue, not a lack of intelligence. But when it becomes deeply rooted, it can become more than just an emotional problem. Physical symptoms appear. Blood pressure may rise and heartbeat may quicken at the sight of a math problem – or even the thought of math! This fear leads to a mental block. When someone with math anxiety is asked to perform a calculation, even a basic problem can seem overwhelming and impossible. The emotional and physical response to the thought of math prevents the brain from working through it logically.

The more this happens, the more a person's confidence drops, and the more math anxiety is generated. This vicious cycle must be broken!

The first step in breaking the cycle is to go back to very beginning and make sure you really understand the basics of how math works and why it works. It is not enough to memorize rules for multiplication and division. If you don't know WHY these rules work, your foundation will be shaky and you will be at risk of developing a phobia. Understanding mathematical concepts not only promotes confidence and security, but allows you to build on this understanding for new concepts. Additionally, you can solve unfamiliar problems using familiar concepts and processes.

Why is it that students in other countries regularly outperform American students in math? The answer likely boils down to a couple of things: the foundation of mathematical conceptual understanding and societal perception. While students in the US are not expected to *like* or *get* math, in many other nations, students are expected not only to understand math but also to excel at it.

Changing the American view of math that leads to math anxiety is a monumental task. It requires changing the training of teachers nationwide, from kindergarten through high school, so that they learn to teach the *why* behind math and to combat the wrong math views that students may develop. It also involves changing the stigma associated with math, so that it is no longer viewed as unpleasant and incomprehensible. While these are necessary changes, they are challenging and will take time. But in the meantime, math anxiety is not irreversible—it can be faced and defeated, one person at a time.

False Beliefs

One reason math anxiety has taken such hold is that several false beliefs have been created and shared until they became widely accepted. Some of these unhelpful beliefs include the following:

There is only one way to solve a math problem. In the same way that you can choose from different driving routes and still arrive at the same house, you can solve a math problem using different methods and still find the correct answer. A person who understands the reasoning behind math calculations may be able to look at an unfamiliar concept and find the right answer, just by applying logic to the knowledge they already have. This approach may be different than what is taught in the classroom, but it is still valid. Unfortunately, even many teachers view math as a subject where the best course of action is to memorize the rule or process for each problem rather than as a place for students to exercise logic and creativity in finding a solution.

Many people don't have a mind for math. A person who has struggled due to poor teaching or math anxiety may falsely believe that he or she doesn't have the mental capacity to grasp mathematical concepts. Most of the time, this is false. Many people find that when they are relieved of their math anxiety, they have more than enough brainpower to understand math.

Men are naturally better at math than women. Even though research has shown this to be false, many young women still avoid math careers and classes because of their belief that their math abilities are inferior. Many girls have come to believe that math is a male skill and have given up trying to understand or enjoy it.

Counting aids are bad. Something like counting on your fingers or drawing out a problem to visualize it may be frowned on as childish or a crutch, but these devices can help you get a tangible understanding of a problem or a concept.

Sadly, many students buy into these ideologies at an early age. A young girl who enjoys math class may be conditioned to think that she doesn't actually have the brain for it because math is for boys, and may turn her energies to other pursuits, permanently closing the door on a wide range of opportunities. A child who finds the right answer but doesn't follow the teacher's method may believe that he is doing it wrong and isn't good at math. A student who never had a problem with math before may have a poor teacher and become confused, yet believe that the problem is because she doesn't have a mathematical mind.

Students who have bought into these erroneous beliefs quickly begin to add their own anxieties, adapting them to their own personal situations:

I'll never use this in real life. A huge number of people wrongly believe that math is irrelevant outside the classroom. By adopting this mindset, they are handicapping themselves for a life in a mathematical world, as well as limiting their career choices. When they are inevitably faced with real-world math, they are conditioning themselves to respond with anxiety.

I'm not quick enough. While timed tests and quizzes, or even simply comparing yourself with other students in the class, can lead to this belief, speed is not an indicator of skill level. A person can work very slowly yet understand at a deep level.

If I can understand it, it's too easy. People with a low view of their own abilities tend to think that if they are able to grasp a concept, it must be simple. They cannot accept the idea that they are capable of understanding math. This belief will make it harder to learn, no matter how intelligent they are.

I just can't learn this. An overwhelming number of people think this, from young children to adults, and much of the time it is simply not true. But this mindset can turn into a self-fulfilling prophecy that keeps you from exercising and growing your math ability.

The good news is, each of these myths can be debunked. For most people, they are based on emotion and psychology, NOT on actual ability! It will take time, effort, and the desire to change, but change is possible. Even if you have spent years thinking that you don't have the capability to understand math, it is not too late to uncover your true ability and find relief from the anxiety that surrounds math.

Math Strategies

It is important to have a plan of attack to combat math anxiety. There are many useful strategies for pinpointing the fears or myths and eradicating them:

Go back to the basics. For most people, math anxiety stems from a poor foundation. You may think that you have a complete understanding of addition and subtraction, or even decimals and percentages, but make absolutely sure. Learning math is different from learning other subjects. For example, when you learn history, you study various time periods and places and events. It may be important to memorize dates or find out about the lives of famous people. When you move from US history to world history, there will be some overlap, but a large amount of the information will be new. Mathematical concepts, on the other hand, are very closely linked and highly dependent on each other. It's like climbing a ladder – if a rung is missing from your understanding, it may be difficult or impossible for you to climb any higher, no matter how hard you try. So go back and make sure your math foundation is strong. This may mean taking a remedial math course, going to a tutor to work through the shaky concepts, or just going through your old homework to make sure you really understand it.

Speak the language. Math has a large vocabulary of terms and phrases unique to working problems. Sometimes these are completely new terms, and sometimes they are common words, but are used differently in a math setting. If you can't speak the language, it will be very difficult to get a thorough understanding of the concepts. It's common for students to think that they don't understand math when they simply don't understand the vocabulary. The good news is that this is fairly easy to fix. Brushing up on any terms you aren't quite sure of can help bring the rest of the concepts into focus.

Check your anxiety level. When you think about math, do you feel nervous or uncomfortable? Do you struggle with feelings of inadequacy, even on concepts that you know you've already learned? It's important to understand your specific math anxieties, and what triggers them. When you catch yourself falling back on a false belief, mentally replace it with the truth. Don't let yourself believe that you can't learn, or that struggling with a concept means you'll never understand it. Instead, remind yourself of how much you've already learned and dwell on that past success. Visualize grasping the new concept, linking it to your old knowledge, and moving on to the next challenge. Also, learn how to manage anxiety when it arises. There are many techniques for coping with the irrational fears that rise to the surface when you enter the math classroom. This may include controlled breathing, replacing negative thoughts with positive ones, or visualizing success. Anxiety interferes with your ability to concentrate and absorb information, which in turn contributes to greater anxiety. If you can learn how to regain control of your thinking, you will be better able to pay attention, make progress, and succeed!

Don't go it alone. Like any deeply ingrained belief, math anxiety is not easy to eradicate. And there is no need for you to wrestle through it on your own. It will take time, and many people find that speaking with a counselor or psychiatrist helps. They can help you develop strategies for responding to anxiety and overcoming old ideas. Additionally, it can be very helpful to take a short course or seek out a math tutor to help you find and fix the missing rungs on your ladder and make sure that you're ready to progress to the next level. You can also find a number of math aids online: courses that will teach you mental devices for figuring out problems, how to get the most out of your math classes, etc.

Check your math attitude. No matter how much you want to learn and overcome your anxiety, you'll have trouble if you still have a negative attitude toward math. If you think it's too hard, or just have general feelings of dread about math, it will be hard to learn and to break through the anxiety. Work on cultivating a positive math attitude. Remind yourself that math is not just a hurdle to be cleared, but a valuable asset. When you view math with a positive attitude, you'll be much more likely to understand and even enjoy it. This is something you must do for yourself. You may find it helpful to visit with a counselor. Your tutor, friends, and family may cheer you on in your endeavors. But your greatest asset is yourself. You are inside your own mind – tell yourself what you need to hear. Relive past victories. Remind yourself that you are capable of understanding math. Root out any false beliefs that linger and replace them with positive truths. Even if it doesn't feel true at first, it will begin to affect your thinking and pave the way for a positive, anxiety-free mindset.

Aside from these general strategies, there are a number of specific practical things you can do to begin your journey toward overcoming math anxiety. Something as simple as learning a new note-taking strategy can change the way you approach math and give you more confidence and understanding. New study techniques can also make a huge difference.

Math anxiety leads to bad habits. If it causes you to be afraid of answering a question in class, you may gravitate toward the back row. You may be embarrassed to ask for help. And you may procrastinate on assignments, which leads to rushing through them at the last moment when it's too late to get a better understanding. It's important to identify your negative behaviors and replace them with positive ones:

Prepare ahead of time. Read the lesson before you go to class. Being exposed to the topics that will be covered in class ahead of time, even if you don't understand them perfectly, is extremely helpful in increasing what you retain from the lecture. Do your homework and, if you're still shaky, go over some extra problems. The key to a solid understanding of math is practice.

Sit front and center. When you can easily see and hear, you'll understand more, and you'll avoid the distractions of other students if no one is in front of you. Plus, you're more likely to be sitting with students who are positive and engaged, rather than others with math anxiety. Let their positive math attitude rub off on you.

Ask questions in class and out. If you don't understand something, just ask. If you need a more in-depth explanation, the teacher may need to work with you outside of class, but often it's a simple concept you don't quite understand, and a single question may clear it up. If you wait, you may not be able to follow the rest of the day's lesson. For extra help, most professors have office hours outside of class when you can go over concepts one-on-one to clear up any uncertainties. Additionally, there may be a *math lab* or study session you can attend for homework help. Take advantage of this.

Review. Even if you feel that you've fully mastered a concept, review it periodically to reinforce it. Going over an old lesson has several benefits: solidifying your understanding, giving you a confidence boost, and even giving some new insights into material that you're currently learning! Don't let yourself get rusty. That can lead to problems with learning later concepts.

Teaching Tips

While the math student's mindset is the most crucial to overcoming math anxiety, it is also important for others to adjust their math attitudes. Teachers and parents have an enormous influence on how students relate to math. They can either contribute to math confidence or math anxiety.

As a parent or teacher, it is very important to convey a positive math attitude. Retelling horror stories of your own bad experience with math will contribute to a new generation of math anxiety. Even if you don't share your experiences, others will be able to sense your fears and may begin to believe them.

Even a careless comment can have a big impact, so watch for phrases like *He's not good at math* or *I never liked math*. You are a crucial role model, and your children or students will unconsciously adopt your mindset. Give them a positive example to follow. Rather than teaching them to fear the math world before they even know it, teach them about all its potential and excitement.

Work to present math as an integral, beautiful, and understandable part of life. Encourage creativity in solving problems. Watch for false beliefs and dispel them. Cross the lines between subjects: integrate history, English, and music with math. Show students how math is used every day, and how the entire world is based on mathematical principles, from the pull of gravity to the shape of seashells. Instead of letting students see math as a necessary evil, direct them to view it as an imaginative, beautiful art form – an art form that they are capable of mastering and using.

Don't give too narrow a view of math. It is more than just numbers. Yes, working problems and learning formulas is a large part of classroom math. But don't let the teaching stop there. Teach students about the everyday implications of math. Show them how nature works according to the laws of mathematics, and take them outside to make discoveries of their own. Expose them to math-related careers by inviting visiting speakers, asking students to do research and presentations, and learning students' interests and aptitudes on a personal level.

Demonstrate the importance of math. Many people see math as nothing more than a required stepping stone to their degree, a nuisance with no real usefulness. Teach students that algebra is used every day in managing their bank accounts, in following recipes, and in scheduling the day's events. Show them how learning to do geometric proofs helps them to develop logical thinking, an invaluable life skill. Let them see that math surrounds them and is integrally linked to their daily lives: that weather predictions are based on math, that math was used to design cars and other machines, etc. Most of all, give them the tools to use math to enrich their lives.

Make math as tangible as possible. Use visual aids and objects that can be touched. It is much easier to grasp a concept when you can hold it in your hands and manipulate it, rather than just listening to the lecture. Encourage math outside of the classroom. The real world is full of measuring, counting, and calculating, so let students participate in this. Keep your eyes open for numbers and patterns to discuss. Talk about how scores are calculated in sports games and how far apart plants are placed in a garden row for maximum growth. Build the mindset that math is a normal and interesting part of daily life.

Finally, find math resources that help to build a positive math attitude. There are a number of books that show math as fascinating and exciting while teaching important concepts, for example: *The Math Curse; A Wrinkle in Time; The Phantom Tollbooth;* and *Fractals, Googols and Other Mathematical Tales.* You can also find a number of online resources: math puzzles and games, videos that show math in nature, and communities of math enthusiasts. On a local level, students can compete in a variety of math competitions with other schools or join a math club.

The student who experiences math as exciting and interesting is unlikely to suffer from math anxiety. Going through life without this handicap is an immense advantage and opens many doors that others have closed through their fear.

Self-Check

Whether you suffer from math anxiety or not, chances are that you have been exposed to some of the false beliefs mentioned above. Now is the time to check yourself for any errors you may have accepted. Do you think you're not wired for math? Or that you don't need to understand it since you're not planning on a math career? Do you think math is just too difficult for the average person?

Find the errors you've taken to heart and replace them with positive thinking. Are you capable of learning math? Yes! Can you control your anxiety? Yes! These errors will resurface from time to time, so be watchful. Don't let others with math anxiety influence you or sway your confidence. If you're having trouble with a concept, find help. Don't let it discourage you!

Create a plan of attack for defeating math anxiety and sharpening your skills. Do some research and decide if it would help you to take a class, get a tutor, or find some online resources to fine-tune your knowledge. Make the effort to get good nutrition, hydration, and sleep so that you are operating at full capacity. Remind yourself daily that you are skilled and that anxiety does not control you. Your mind is capable of so much more than you know. Give it the tools it needs to grow and thrive.

Thank You

We at Mometrix would like to extend our heartfelt thanks to you, our friend and patron, for allowing us to play a part in your journey. It is a privilege to serve people from all walks of life who are unified in their commitment to building the best future they can for themselves.

The preparation you devote to these important testing milestones may be the most valuable educational opportunity you have for making a real difference in your life. We encourage you to put your heart into it—that feeling of succeeding, overcoming, and yes, conquering will be well worth the hours you've invested.

We want to hear your story, your struggles and your successes, and if you see any opportunities for us to improve our materials so we can help others even more effectively in the future, please share that with us as well. **The team at Mometrix would be absolutely thrilled to hear from you!** So please, send us an email (support@mometrix.com) and let's stay in touch.

If you'd like some additional help, check out these other resources we offer for your exam:

http://MometrixFlashcards.com/NYStateTests

Additional Bonus Material

Due to our efforts to try to keep this book to a manageable length, we've created a link that will give you access to all of your additional bonus material.

Please visit http://www.mometrix.com/bonus948/nystg4sci to access the information.